Michelle Wie

Other books in the People in the News series:

Maya Angelou

Tyra Banks

Glenn Beck

David Beckham

Beyoncé

Fidel Castro

Kelly Clarkson

Hillary Clinton

Miley Cyrus

Ellen Degeneres

Leonardo DiCaprio

Hilary Duff

Zac Efron

Brett Favre

50 Cent

Jeff Gordon

Al Gore

Tony Hawk

Salma Hayek

LeBron James

Jay-Z

Derek Jeter

Steve Jobs

Dwayne Johnson

Angelina Jolie

Jonas Brothers

Kim Jong II

Coretta Scott King

Ashton Kutcher

Spike Lee

George Lopez

Tobey Maguire

Eli Manning

John McCain

Barack Obama

Michelle Obama

Danica Patrick

Nancy Pelosi

Tyler Perry

Queen Latifah

Daniel Radcliffe

Condoleezza Rice

Rihanna

Alex Rodriguez

Derrick Rose

J.K. Rowling

Shakira

Tupac Shakur

Will Smith

Gwen Stefani

Ben Stiller

Hilary Swank

Justin Timberlake

Usher

Denzel Washington

Serena Williams

Oprah Winfrey

Michelle Wie

by Lauri Scherer

LUCENT BOOKS

A part of Gale, Cengage Learning

GALE
CENGAGE Learning·

Detroit • New York • San Francisco • New Haven, Conn • Waterville, Maine • London

LIBRARY OF CONGRESS CATALOGING-IN-PUBLICATION DATA

Scherer, Laurie.
  Michelle Wie / Laurie Scherer.
    p. cm. -- (People in the news)
  Summary: "This series profiles the lives and careers of some of today's most promi-
nent newsmakers. Whether covering contributions and achievements or notorious
deeds, books in this series examine why these well-known personages garnered public
attention"-- Provided by publisher.
  Includes bibliographical references and index.
  ISBN 978-1-4205-0610-5 (hardback)
1. Wie, Michelle. 2. Golfers--United States--Biography. 3. Women golfers--United
States--Biography. I. Title.
  GV964.W49S34 2011
  796.352092--dc23
  [B]
                                                                            2011018026

Lucent Books
27500 Drake Rd
Farmington Hills MI 48331

ISBN-13: 978-1-4205-0610-5
ISBN-10: 1-4205-0610-2

Printed in the United States of America
1 2 3 4 5 6 7 15 14 13 12 11

Printed by Bang Printing, Brainerd, MN, 1st Ptg., 08/2011

Contents

ame and celebrity are alluring. People are drawn to those who walk in fame's spotlight, whether they are known for great accomplishments or for notorious deeds. The lives of the famous pique public interest and attract attention, perhaps because their experiences seem in some ways so different from, yet in other ways so similar to, our own.

Newspapers, magazines, and television regularly capitalize on this fascination with celebrity by running profiles of famous people. For example, television programs such as *Entertainment Tonight* devote all their programming to stories about entertainment and entertainers. Magazines such as *People* fill their pages with stories of the private lives of famous people. Even newspapers, newsmagazines, and television news frequently delve into the lives of well-known personalities. Despite the number of articles and programs, few provide more than a superficial glimpse at their subjects.

Lucent's People in the News series offers young readers a deeper look into the lives of today's newsmakers, the influences that have shaped them, and the impact they have had in their fields of endeavor and on other people's lives. The subjects of the series hail from many disciplines and walks of life. They include authors, musicians, athletes, political leaders, entertainers, entrepreneurs, and others who have made a mark on modern life and who, in many cases, will continue to do so for years to come.

These biographies are more than factual chronicles. Each book emphasizes the contributions, accomplishments, or deeds that have brought fame or notoriety to the individual and shows how that person has influenced modern life. Authors portray their subjects in a realistic, unsentimental light. For example, Bill Gates—the cofounder of the software giant Microsoft—has been instrumental in making personal computers the most vital tool of the modern age. Few dispute his business savvy, his perseverance, or his technical expertise, yet critics say he is ruthless in his dealings with competitors and driven more by his desire to maintain Microsoft's dominance in the computer industry than by an interest in furthering technology.

In these books, young readers will encounter inspiring stories about real people who achieved success despite enormous obstacles. Oprah Winfrey—one of the most powerful, most watched, and wealthiest women in television history—spent the first six years of her life in the care of her grandparents while her unwed mother sought work and a better life elsewhere. Her adolescence was colored by pregnancy at age fourteen, rape, and sexual abuse.

Each author documents and supports his or her work with an array of primary and secondary source quotations taken from diaries, letters, speeches, and interviews. All quotes are footnoted to show readers exactly how and where biographers derive their information and provide guidance for further research. The quotations enliven the text by giving readers eyewitness views of the life and accomplishments of each person covered in the People in the News series.

In addition, each book in the series includes photographs, annotated bibliographies, timelines, and comprehensive indexes. For both the casual reader and the student researcher, the People in the News series offers insight into the lives of today's newsmakers—people who shape the way we live, work, and play in the modern age.

"I Don't Want to Be Normal"

It was difficult to guess what a young Michelle Wie might be thinking as she dangled her feet a few inches above the floor of the golf cart. It is safe to say that most ten-year-olds probably do not think about how bored they get beating their mother, a former South Korean women's amateur golf champion, at golf. Most ten-year-olds probably have not reflected on how they are the youngest player in history ever to qualify for the U.S. Women's Amateur Public Links Championship, either. Most have never looked ahead to the Hawaii State Women's Stroke Play Championship and the Jennie K. Wilson Women's Invitational— events that Michelle won at the age of eleven—with the anticipation of a kid on her way to Disneyland. In fact, most ten-year-olds have never even played golf.

Michelle Wie has never been like most kids, though, and she has always known it. "I guess if you grow up normal, you'll always be normal," she said. "And I don't want to be normal. I want to be something else."[1]

Wie has challenged the meaning of *normal* her whole life: Few elements of her story fit into tidy, predictable boxes. Depending on which point in Wie's career they were written, various newspaper and magazine articles about her seem to describe the lives and accomplishments of entirely different young women. Some see her as a supremely talented, highly focused golfing sensation; the Tiger Woods of women's golf. Others view her as a young phenomenon, robbed of a childhood, who suffered from experiencing too much, too soon. Still others have described Wie as a burned-out prodigy, a fluke, an overhyped player. The truth is probably somewhere in between.

A True Standout

Wie's impact on the golf world began long before her amateur career did in 2000. She first received attention locally when she tagged along to play golf with her parents at their golf course in Hawaii. Spectators were interested in her before she ever entered a single tournament. Her smooth, powerful swing was compared to that of a seasoned professional when she was only ten years old. Once she began showcasing her skills in amateur tournaments, it became clear that not only did she have a talent for swinging the club well, but she also had a genuine understanding of golf. She excited audiences by declaring her intention to play someday with—and even beat—male golfers. She did not win every tournament she entered, but her remarkable grasp of the game at such a young age made her a true standout.

In the early years of her professional career, however, it was a series of dismal failures and embarrassing mistakes that made her stand out. Indeed, her first few years as a professional golfer were chaotic and unsteady, a surprising turn for someone who showed so much potential in her preteen years. "There were times when Wie simply dazzled," wrote sports reporter Doug Ferguson as he reflected on her first season as a pro golfer, "and there were times when everyone wondered what in the world Wie was doing."[2] Fans, sports journalists, and other commentators had almost more to say about Wie's floundering than they did about her initial success. Some reporters seemed willing to write her epitaph before she was even eighteen years old. "She's ancient history," said sports columnist Tim Dahlberg. "At age 17, she can't find the fairway with her driver, and the idea of competing against the men seems laughable when she can't even beat her own gender."[3]

A comeback in 2009 restored the public's faith in Wie, and her faith in herself. Winning her first professional tournament that year helped people remember why she had turned heads

Michelle Wie has grown from child prodigy into a successful professional with accomplishments both on and off the golf course.

in the first place. As she entered her early twenties, Wie had accomplished more than most people do in an entire lifetime. As of 2011 Wie was standing out for all the right reasons: her ability to handle both success and failure, her willingness to meet challenges head on, her success at one of the premier colleges in the United States, and her indelible mark on the sport of golf. Her future looked bright, and it was easier to remember why the world had become enchanted with her in the first place. Mike Whan, commissioner of the Ladies Professional Golf Association, is one of many who realize that for all of Wie's ups and downs, she is still at the beginning of what is likely to be a very long career. "Because we've heard about Michelle Wie for so long, you forget that she's [so young]," said Whan. "Her best golf is ahead of her."[4]

Chapter 1

A Childhood Rooted in Success

Michelle Sung Wie was born on October 11, 1989, in Honolulu, Hawaii. She is the only child of Byung-Wook (B.J.) and Hyun-Kyong (Bo) Wie, both of whom immigrated to the United States from South Korea. B.J. came to California in 1983 and met Bo in Los Angeles in 1987. The couple got married and moved to Honolulu in 1988, where they were able to secure jobs fairly easily, given both B.J.'s and Bo's natural intelligence and drive for success. B.J. got a job as a transportation professor at the University of Hawaii. Bo became a successful realtor. Comfortable in their jobs and ready to begin a family, they welcomed their only child into the world the following year and named her Michelle, after the popular Beatles song of the same name.

B.J. and Bo were both tall, so it is not surprising that Michelle was a large baby. Most babies are 18 to 20 inches (45.7 to 50.8 cm) long at birth, but Michelle measured a remarkable 22 inches (55.9cm) at birth. She had an unusually large head and unusually large hands and feet. Aside from being a large baby, she was also quite strong, in every sense of the word, from the day she was born. Before she was two weeks old, she could push her head and upper body away from the bed or from whomever was holding her. By the time she was a few months old, she had a hefty appetite and could eat two to three times as much as most babies her age. At an age when most babies were learning to turn over, Michelle could rock her body and scoot from one place to

The Republic of Korea

Otherwise known as South Korea, the Republic of Korea is a small country located in East Asia. It is the birthplace of Michelle's parents, Bo and B.J. Wie, and a place to which Michelle feels strongly connected.

The South Korean capital is the heavily populated and bustling city of Seoul. The current president is Lee Myung-bak. The country has a long and rich history that is marked by the Japanese occupation of Korea, which ended with Japan's defeat in World War II in 1945. From then on, Korea was divided but experienced major turmoil until the establishment of two separate governments, which eventually stabilized into the two separate entities of North and South Korea.

Since it came into existence, South Korea has enjoyed substantial economic and educational development. The country has risen from one of Asia's poorest to one of the world's wealthiest nations.

another. At just nine months she could walk, and shortly after, she was running from place to place as fast as her sturdy legs could carry her.

Early Signs of Excellence

Michelle was advanced in many other ways as well. For instance, she began learning her letters while other babies were still learning to play peek-a-boo. Soon she was able to read words and simple sentences. "I learned most of the letters of the alphabet before I turned one and learned to read before I turned two," she says. "My parents are so proud of that." She also has an early memory of being able to read complete sentences and signs: "My very first memory is going down by the pool in the apartment where we lived and reading the sign that said, 'Warning: Don't

Wie poses with her father, B.J., left, and mother, Bo, in 2002. The Wies, avid golfers themselves, introduced their daughter to the sport when she was four years old.

dive.' I didn't know what it meant, but I could read it and knew it had something to do with danger."[5]

Since Michelle was born into an athletic and sports-loving family, it was only natural that some of her childhood play would involve different kinds of sports. When she first learned to walk and run, her parents would roll tennis balls across the floor of her father's office and watch her scurry after them. B.J. and Bo were amazed at how quickly their young toddler picked up new skills and also at how much information she retained. It was fun for them to test what Michelle was capable of.

B.J. and Bo made further discoveries about their daughter's skills via their interest in golf. Bo had been South Korea's women's amateur golf champion in 1985, and B.J. enjoyed the game as well. Golf ran in Michelle's family, and her parents were excited to introduce her to the sport. In 1994, when she was a little over four years old, Michelle's father took her to a park in Honolulu. As they walked across the baseball field that sunny day, B.J. carried a few golf balls and one of his own mother's old golf clubs. He had cut the club down to a smaller size to fit Michelle better.

When B.J. and Michelle reached the middle of the field, he placed one of the balls on the ground and handed Michelle the small club. He did not tell her how to stand or how to swing. He just wanted to see what she would do. She grabbed the club, posed in a good imitation of the familiar golf swing posture, looked at the ball, and took her very first swing. To her father's utter surprise, she successfully connected with the ball and smashed it all the way to the outfield.

The Littlest Golfer

Although B.J. suspected his young daughter was gifted, he did not expect such success the very first time his four-year-old got her hands on a golf club. Michelle was happy with the reaction her big swing got from her father. Every time she hit the ball, she swung so hard she nearly fell over, which further intrigued B.J. "Michelle has always liked to hit the ball hard," B.J. later said of Michelle's early abilities. "Sometimes it would go right, sometimes left, but it didn't matter. She just wanted to hit the ball hard."[6] On this day in the park, B.J. saw something special in his daughter.

Wie and her father, B.J., study a shot at a tournament in 2003. The power of Wie's swing was apparent from early childhood, when she started shooting golf balls in her family's backyard.

Shortly after B.J. and Bo discovered their daughter had incredible coordination, strength, and talent for hitting golf balls, the family moved from an apartment to a house. Instead of playing with dolls or dressing up in her mother's clothes like many little girls do, Michelle spent much of her time whacking golf balls around the backyard. As Michelle's swing improved, the balls reached greater and greater distances. When she was five years old, Michelle could drive a ball 100 yards (91.44m). Everyone in the neighborhood started taking notice, especially when Michelle's shots began to land outside the perimeter of the Wie's yard. Her drives sent the balls into neighbors' yards—and occasionally through their windows. The neighbors began to complain. They feared for their safety as well as for their windows, patio doors, and other breakable objects on their property. Finally, although she was still very young, Michelle's parents could see no choice but to take her along to the golf course, where she could hit the

Other Famous Athletic Child Prodigies

Michelle Wie belongs to an elite group of famous athletic superstars who were also considered child prodigies. Fellow golfer Tiger Woods is one of them. He started golfing before the age of two and was coached by his father, Earl. In 1984, at the age of eight, he won a tournament at the Junior World Golf Championships in the age 9–10 boys' event, the youngest category in the championship. He first broke a score of 80 at age eight and went on to win the Junior World Championships six times.

Tiger Woods, a golf prodigy like Wie who went on to dominate the sport as an adult, competes in a tournament at age fourteen.

Hockey great Wayne Gretzky, often considered the greatest hockey player in the history of the National Hockey League, is another athletic prodigy. Gretzky started skating with ten-year-olds at the age of six, which set the precedent for him to play at a level far above his peers through his minor hockey years. By ten years old, he had scored 378 goals and 139 assists in just 85 games with the Nadrofsky Steelers.

Skateboarder and snowboarder Shaun White is another athletic prodigy. White was discovered by skateboarding legend Tony Hawk when he was just nine years old. He became a professional skateboarder at age seventeen and went on to win the title of Action Sports Tour Champion. He has won both the Summer and Winter X Games (in both snowboarding and skateboarding). He also won gold medals for snowboarding in both the 2006 and 2010 Winter Olympics.

ball with total freedom and also learn some other aspects of the game. Michelle was not quite seven years old when she stepped on her first golf course.

Hitting the Course with Michelle

B.J. and Bo Wie were members at a local course called the Olomana Golf Links. Conveniently located about fifteen minutes from their home, they played as often as possible. Michelle's presence at the golf club quickly generated controversy among the

A Long History of Wie Achievement

The Wie family has a long history of achievement. Michelle's great-grandfather was a scholar and teacher of the Chinese language. His son, Michelle's grandfather, Sang-Kyu Wie, fought in the Korean War in the early 1950s. He was a South Korean fighter pilot who flew nearly one hundred combat missions with the American forces against North Korea and China. Sang-Kyu Wie earned several medals from the American armed forces, including the Distinguished Flying Cross.

After the war, Sang-Kyu and his wife, Kyung-Hee, moved to the United States while Sang-Kyu furthered his education. In 1959 Sang-Kyu earned his PhD in aerospace engineering at the University of Minnesota. He was the first Korean ever to receive this degree in the United States.

Michelle's father, Byung-Wook (B.J.), first attended university in Seoul, but like his father, moved to the United States to complete his education. He received his PhD in transportation science at the University of Pennsylvania in the early 1980s. Michelle's mother, Hyun-Kyong (Bo), was also successful. Before moving to California to go to school, she was the reigning Miss Korea.

other members, however. Many felt a golf course was a place for adults only. They worried the little girl would make noise, interrupt or delay their games, and generally change the atmosphere of the club. It took just a few times of seeing Michelle in action before most changed their minds. Michelle was not there to play around but to play golf, and thus she quickly fit right in.

Although Michelle was tall for her age, the club's starter (the person who decides where and when golfers tee off, or start their game) could tell she was young—maybe too young to play the course. When she told him she was just seven, he was hesitant to let her on the links (a type of course built on or near the coast). She was so persistent, however, that he finally partnered her with an older woman. The woman was not happy to have a child for a partner and reluctantly agreed to play with her. Soon, though, the woman was unhappy for another reason: Michelle easily outscored her. The woman left the course in disgust after completing only nine holes. The other golfers soon learned that Michelle did not need to get out of their way: *they* needed to get out of *hers*.

In addition to learning the rules of golf, Michelle was learning other aspects of the game, too. Golf has a particular culture associated with it, and Michelle quickly learned what clothing is appropriate on the course, when it is appropriate to talk and when it is not, and other key course etiquette. Not only was Michelle hitting the ball far and outplaying many of the adult members, she was learning to look and act the part as well. The sport of golf has a specific etiquette, a set of rules and customs regarding dress and behavior. For example, jeans are not allowed on most courses; shirts need to be collared and tucked in. Also, when another player is teeing off, putting, or taking any other shot, absolute silence is required. Bo and B.J. taught Michelle what to wear and how to act on the course.

Michelle's interest in golf was firmly established by the time she was seven. It was then that she played her first full, eighteen-hole round of golf, and she scored well. In golf each hole is given a number called a "par," which is the number of strokes it should take a golfer to finish that hole. For example, if a hole is designated as par 4, and a golfer gets the ball into the hole in five strokes, then the score for that hole would be 1 over par. At the end of each hole, the number of strokes is counted and the number over or under par is determined (if a golfer gets the ball in the hole in the same number of strokes as the hole's par, he or she gets a zero for that hole—so four strokes on a par 4 would result in a score of zero for the hole). At the end of the game, the strokes for all holes are tallied for the final score. Golf is one of the few games where the goal is to get a low score instead of a high one.

On Michelle's first eighteen-hole round of golf, she scored 14 over par. This was a phenomenal score. Not only was this a great score for a seven-year-old child, but it was a score many adults would envy, too.

A Different Kind of Childhood

Excelling at a mature sport like golf was just one of the things that made Michelle's childhood different. Michelle had posters on her bedroom walls as other kids do, except instead of posters of actors and rock bands, her walls were covered with posters of her golf idols, such as Tiger Woods. Michelle also sometimes watched television, but rather than just watching cartoons and other kids' programs, she watched the Professional Golfers Association (PGA) and Ladies Professional Golf Association (LPGA) tours. Michelle liked activities more typical of a child her age, too, however. She liked to play Digimon and Pokémon video games, and she enjoyed reading, especially Laura Ingalls Wilder's *Little House on the Prairie*. She also played on her school's softball team and, because of her powerful swing, excelled at tennis. In fact, for a brief time, the Wies thought that tennis would be Michelle's main sport because she was so good at it.

But nothing intrigued Michelle as much as golf. As she studied the swings of all the best golfers she saw on TV, she found herself more interested in the men's hitting styles than the women's. She wanted to play a strong, powerful game like the men, rather than a refined, graceful one typical of the female players. She made it clear to her parents and anyone else who would listen that she intended to play against men one day. Michelle once said, "I watch ... the PGA tour, not the LPGA. I like the players

Wie shoots a practice round under the watchful eye of her parents, who supported their daughter's passion for golf from an early age.

on the PGA better. I want to play on the PGA tour."[7] This, too, was a unique dream for a young girl.

Her parents were supportive of Michelle's dreams, yet careful not to push too hard. They did not force her to play golf or other sports, nor did they impose limitations on her in the sports she chose to play. They did not tell her that women were not allowed to play against men in competition, so she just assumed that she would one day have male opponents. She also assumed she would play well enough to beat some of them.

Michelle's First Coach

For the next few years, B.J. acted as his daughter's coach and caddie. Michelle was a fast and focused learner, however, and before long, B.J. taught her all he knew. Michelle not only needed better instruction, she needed more of a challenge to keep her game sharp. By the time she was nine years old, the Wies' tall, dynamo daughter was outscoring both of her parents just about every time they played together. Since she knew she would probably beat them, playing with her parents was starting to bore her. Realizing Michelle needed professional training and more skilled opponents, they began the search for a professional coach.

B.J. and Bo did not have to look far. They quickly discovered one-time professional golfer Casey Nakama, owner of the Casey Nakama Golf Development Center at the Olomana Golf Links, where the Wies were members. Nakama was used to parents bringing him their children in the hopes he would recognize their talent and push them to the next level of play. In Nakama's opinion, most of those children were not exceptionally talented. He saw something truly different in Michelle, however. He was taken aback by her size and strength. What really caught his eye, though, was her determination. "She was so driven at what she did," he remembers. "Even at 10 years old, she didn't mind practicing every day. She was just determined to do whatever we were working on. We would make a swing adjustment, and she would work on it and come back in three or four days and say, 'I think I got it, Casey.' That work ethic, it separates her from a lot of the other players."[8]

In the beginning Nakama focused Michelle on relearning golf so he could make absolutely sure that she learned everything correctly. He watched her play and observed her technique. Although Michelle's swing was powerful and impressive, she sometimes failed to control the strength in her swing; her game needed refining on several levels. Nakama taught her to point her club at the target at the top of her backswing in order to send her ball exactly where she wanted it to go. He showed her how to hold a good grip and how to stand so her posture was appropriately angled relative to the ball. He also taught her how to control distance

Wie lines up a putt while her father looks on. B.J. taught his daughter the game until he determined that she needed a professional coach in order to further develop her skills.

when she hit the ball. He taught her other skills of the game as well, such as putting, hitting the ball out of the rough (the thick grassy area on the outskirts of the course), player positioning (where to stand while hitting the ball or observing a partner's play), and how to keep the pace of the game moving, which is a key part of golf.

Michelle practiced her new stance and swing in front of a huge mirror. She practiced for hours on the links, until both student and coach were satisfied. She had natural talent, but she also practiced extremely hard for such a young girl. Her game eventually got so good that Nakama decided she was ready to play in a competition.

Ready for Competition

By the time she was in fifth grade, her father and coach Nakama decided it was time to test Michelle in an actual golf competition. Her first was the 1999 Oahu Junior Championship. She did well for the first part of the round, but despite having a big lead, she made some critical mistakes. In the end Michelle showed her tenacity and determination—she pushed through and put the ball 3 inches (7.62cm) from the cup, and won.

Not only did this win set the tone for a string of local and junior wins for Michelle. It also made her realize that golf was not only fun; it was also about winning. She was motivated by the thrill of competition. "After a while, once we got her into some competitions, then she liked [golf] even more, she liked competing because it tested her skills," said Nakama. "Even at 11 years old, she got really intense."[9]

Her thirst for competition led Michelle to ask Nakama if she could play against older golfers. Nakama would sometimes let Michelle play against some of the older boys at the links, but the boys quickly lost interest in being routinely beaten by a little girl. Michelle's interest in the game, however, only continued to grow. Michelle increased her practice time, squeezing in practices every day after school. Her mom would pick her up and drive her to Olomana. Michelle did her homework in the car on the ride over. Bo often caddied her practice rounds with Nakama while her

As an adolescent, Wie's outstanding skills were matched by her competitive nature. She enjoyed early success in tournament play as well as in matches against older boys.

father observed and took notes. During summer break, Michelle would hit the links at 9:30 each morning to play eighteen holes, and then practice until it got dark. Getting an eleven-year-old to practice anything for a substantial amount of time is a challenge for most parents, but Michelle never complained about the long hours she spent on the course. In fact, she loved it.

Nakama and Michelle's parents feared that if they did not feed her desire for more, she would get bored with winning and, eventually, bored with golf. While it seemed unfathomable that such a young girl could already have outgrown playing her parents, older boys, and also junior-level tournaments, Nakama could not deny that this was happening. It was time to see what else Michelle could do by taking her game to the next level.

Chapter 2

Little Girl, Big Wins

As Coach Nakama searched out a more challenging event for Michelle, he looked beyond Hawaii and sets his sights on the mainland. He entered Michelle in the U.S. Women's Amateur Public Links championship in North Carolina in 2000, when she was just ten years old. As a result, Michelle became the youngest player ever to compete for a women's U.S. Golf Association (USGA) title. This experience launched Michelle's amateur career. During this time she did not win every tournament she entered, but her smooth, powerful swing made her one of the youngest and most powerful players, and also one of the most watched.

Michelle's appearance in the mainland event caught the eye of local and national media outlets. The young prodigy fascinated journalists. Being asked to reflect on her skills and swing made Michelle realize that she was truly a rare talent. It also thrust her into the spotlight in a new and sometimes uncomfortable way. Nobody had ever asked her questions about her practice schedule or routines before. Her parents worried she was too young for such exposure, or that media attention would distract her from her game. They therefore tried to shield Michelle from the media as much as they could, even turning down an offer for her to appear on *The Tonight Show with Jay Leno*. She was, however, allowed to speak to the media in small doses. When asked by a journalist who her golf idol was, for example, she said it was Tiger Woods. When asked if she thought she could beat him, Michelle earnestly replied, "Maybe when I'm fifteen."[10]

Michelle Wie's Power Drink

Michelle Wie credits her success to her hard work, focus, and natural talent. She also gets some help from a special "juice" her mother makes for her every day. The juice is a homemade mixture of herbs, ginseng, and boiled goat's meat. Michelle says it "tastes like coffee and vomit," but Bo claims it makes her strong and gives her all the nutrition and stamina she needs to practice for hours. The drink has been rumored to include everything from deer antlers to snakes to magical herbs. Michelle and Bo deny these are included, but do say they occasionally switch up the ingredients.

Quoted in "The Club Kid," *People*, June 30, 2003, p. 132.
www.people.com/people/archive/article/0,,20140447,00.html.

A Winning Streak

As Michelle entered her second decade, she embarked on an impressive winning streak. The next few years were marked by several crucial and record-breaking victories for her. At age eleven she won the Hawaii State Women's Stroke Play Championship, becoming the youngest winner in history. In May that same year, she won the Jennie K. Wilson Women's Invitational, the most prestigious women's amateur tournament in Hawaii. Again, she was the youngest winner in the history of the event. This was a massive victory for Michelle— winning such a highly respected tournament meant that more and bigger opportunities were likely to come her way.

That proved true in June 2001 when she became the youngest golfer and first female to qualify for the Ninety-Third Manoa Cup Hawaii State Amateur Match Play Championship, an event that has traditionally been played by men and has been held since the early 1900s. She also won the Hawaii State Junior Golf Association's Tournament of Champions in 2001 and 2002. Also in

Wie hits a tee shot as the youngest golfer ever to qualify for an LPGA Tour event at the 2002 Takefuji Classic in Waikoloa, Hawaii.

2002, Michelle qualified for the Takefuji Classic, part of the LPGA Tour. This was her first LPGA Tour event, and she made history by becoming the youngest golfer to qualify for an LPGA event.

The PGA Versus the LPGA

A woman playing on the PGA Tour usually attracts a lot of media attention. This is not because women are not allowed to play on the PGA—the PGA is for all pro golfers, both men and women, who are good enough to play the tougher courses. Rather, few female golfers are able to hit the long drives needed to tee off from the PGA tees. Hitting the ball from these tees makes the course considerably longer and more difficult, and thus the PGA attracts mostly male players.

Golf superstar Annika Sörenstam, right, takes to the practice range with her male competitors at a PGA Tour event in 2003.

If she can make these long drives, however, a female player has several reasons to try to play on the PGA. For one, the prize money on that tour is considerably more than on the LPGA Tour. Also, some women golfers, like the Swedish-born Annika Sörenstam, have defeated most of the top women golfers and seek out the challenge of playing with men.

Another difference between the PGA and the LPGA is that there are far more winners of the PGA Tour. On the LPGA Tour, however, the same core of women usually ends up winning the events.

Michelle played in two other LPGA events in 2002 and scored well enough to advance to the Wendy's Championship for Children in August. She missed the cut, however, in part because she received a two-stroke penalty for playing too slowly (in golf tournaments, the top scorers in the initial rounds are selected, or "make the cut," to advance to the final rounds, where prize money is awarded). Why she suffered this penalty was a matter of debate among spectators, but it was believed that as Michelle's caddie, her father was dissecting her shots with her on the tees. The distraction probably significantly and critically slowed down her game. The incident caused some to suggest it might be time for Michelle to get an official caddie instead of using her father, whose heavy investment in his daughter's success might end up being a distraction for her. However, she was so young that most supporters felt it was still appropriate for her father to accompany Michelle on the course.

Wie's victories continued throughout 2002 when she became the youngest junior medalist of the Trans National Women's Amateur Championship and the youngest player to advance to the semifinals of the USGA Women's Amateur Public Links Championship (though she lost to fellow Korean Hwanhee Lee). In her final event in 2002, Michelle won the Women's Division of the Hawaii State Open by thirteen strokes, a clear and strong triumph for such a young golfer.

Michelle's extraordinary talent earned her the respect of older professional golfers before she was even in the sixth grade. Fred Couples, winner of several PGA tournaments, including the highly respected Masters Tournament, once remarked, "When you see her hit a golf ball … there's nothing that prepares you for it. It's just the scariest thing you've ever seen."[11] Australian golfer Karrie Webb agreed, saying, "I'm in awe of someone like Michelle Wie, because of how good she is at a young age."[12]

A New Coach

Michelle kept herself busy during her preteen years by winning as many competitions as she could. As their daughter progressed, B.J. and Bo decided it was time for her to develop a relationship

Wie warms up before the 2003 Nationwide Tour Boise Open with some practice drives under the direction of Gary Gilchirst, left, who became her coach in 2002.

with a new coach. Nakama had taught young Michelle for nearly three years and was very close to the Wies. He nurtured Michelle's talent during what is arguably the most crucial time in a young athlete's life. Michelle had reached a turning point in her game, however, and Michelle's parents thought she would benefit from the direction of golfer Gary Gilchrist.

Gilchrist is a former professional golfer from South Africa, a country that is known for producing great golfers such as Ernie Els. In 1994 Gilchrist moved to the United States upon being offered a job in Florida at the famous David Leadbetter Golf Academy. He was the director of golf at the academy when he met Michelle in February 2002. Their story was more one of chance, as Gilchrist was in Honolulu leading a coaching seminar. He placed a key phone call to the Wie family in which he offered to work with Michelle. His focus was junior golf, so Michelle seemed like the perfect student for his instruction. When Gilchrist witnessed Michelle's strength and skill in person, he was taken aback: "I've seen a lot of juniors come through. At 12 years old, she had the power and the finesse, components I have never seen on a kid like that before. She naturally just hit the ball ... the driving range was 250 yards long and she was flying the fence."[13]

The Wie family traveled to Florida to work with Gilchrist for weeks at a time in 2002 and early 2003. Gilchrist believed in Michelle's talent and was excited by the attention she was bringing to junior golf and to women's golf in general. "[Michelle] is getting a lot of kids, especially girls, into the game of golf,"[14] he noted.

Continuing the Climb

In 2003, under Gilchrist's instruction, thirteen-year-old Michelle was hungry to make even more of a mark on the golf world. That year, at the Twenty-Fifth Anniversary Hawaii Pearl Open, she became the first and youngest female to make the cut, then tied for a forty-third-place finish.

It was on the 2003 LPGA Tour that she really dominated, however. She tied for ninth place at the Kraft Nabisco Championship, an achievement that broke numerous records, including youngest player to make the cut at an LPGA event (thirteen years, five months, seventeen days) and youngest player to finish in the top ten at an LPGA event (thirteen years, five months, nineteen days). Later that summer, she made the cut at the U.S. Women's Open when she was still just thirteen, the youngest player ever to do so.

Wie really made her mark in June 2003, however, when she won the U.S. Women's Amateur Public Links tournament. She defeated a tough Thai competitor, Virada Nirapathpongporn, and became the youngest person, male or female, ever to win a USGA adult event. Winning the tournament and making the cut at the U.S. Women's Open proved to the world that despite her age, Michelle was a force to be reckoned with.

Michelle's steady climb to success in the golf world earned her other notable accomplishments. The 2004 Sony Open in Hawaii marked a big milestone for Michelle. She was given a sponsor's exemption to the event. A sponsor's exemption is when a tournament sponsor invites nonmember players, usually amateurs, to play in an event because they can increase ticket sales, media attention, and visibility. Her inclusion in the event made her just the fourth, and the youngest, female ever to play a PGA Tour event. This was a big chance for her to prove herself to the public, so the Wies wanted to put Michelle in the best position

Wie listens to advice from Ernie Els, left, during a practice round at the 2004 Sony Open. Els, one of Wie's golfing idols, offered her tips on putting that helped her improve that part of her game.

to win. Instead of B.J. being her caddie for the event, they hired a professional caddie. Although she did not win, she got a 68 in the second round, which broke the record for the lowest score achieved by any woman player in a PGA Tour event.

The media attention surrounding Michelle was intense. Reporters watched her every swing as she nervously tried to do well in the men's event. While she did not end up placing very high (and did not actually make the cut for the tournament), she did beat several of her male opponents, some of whom were previous PGA champions, a feat noted by sportswriter David Lefort. "Listen up, guys: Wie beat 48 players with her even-par 140 score, including five whom won on the PGA Tour in 2003. ... She also finished tied with two of last year's major champions. ... Not too shabby," wrote Lefort. "Next up for the 14-year-old Wie is a return to ninth grade, but we'll be seeing her again soon."[15]

Michelle also received some key advice from an important person at the Sony Open. During a practice round before the tournament started, legendary golfer and one of Michelle's

Michelle's Golf Heroes

Two of Michelle's all-time favorite golfers are Tiger Woods and Ernie Els. Because Woods is frequently in the media spotlight, much is known about his golf abilities and accomplishments. Ernie Els is less known but is equally talented.

Originally from South Africa, Els won several major tournaments from the mid-1990s through the early 2000s, including the U.S. Open in 1994 and 1997 as well as the Open Championship in 2002. He has held the number one spot in the Official World Golf Rankings and holds the record for number of weeks ranked in the top ten. In 2010, he was added to the World Golf Hall of Fame. His tall stature and graceful, powerful swing have earned him the nickname "The Big Easy," from which Wie's nickname is derived.

personal idols, Ernie Els, came over to Michelle. He told her that on long putts, she tended to rush her putter to the ball too quickly. Els told her to think of her putter as a pendulum and to relax and not force her swing. Els's advice was very helpful. Michelle was known for her big drives, but her short game, the part of the game in which a golfer putts to get the ball in the hole, sometimes suffered. After hearing Els's advice, she greatly improved this aspect of her game: She took only twelve putts on her last ten holes and missed becoming the youngest person to make the cut at a PGA Tour event by only one stroke. In June 2004, at fourteen, Michelle also became part of the youngest squad in history to play a two-day event called the Curtis Cup, which occurs every two years. The team's average age was about eighteen.

As Michelle grew up playing in the public spotlight, not only did she develop into a strong and highly competitive golfer, but she also grew to over 6 feet (183cm) tall and developed super-model good looks. She was talented, good-looking, and fun to watch, which made her an immediate magnet for tournament officials and corporate sponsors. Because Michelle attracted fan and media attention, her presence at tournaments helped sell tickets. That she appealed to a younger audience was also important to those looking to capitalize on her popularity.

Signature Golf Swing

In addition to her crowd appeal, Michelle was fast becoming known for her powerful golf swing. Some marveled at the distances she could reach, while others admired the technical skill and the beauty in her stroke. Michelle's swing was aided by her size. In addition to being tall, she was rumored to wear a men's size 9.5 shoe and had incredibly long arms and legs, which are great tools for perfecting a powerful swing. David Leadbetter, of the David Leadbetter Golf Academy, noted that Michelle's height was an asset to her as she developed her swing. "For a tall player, Michelle has superb posture," he said. "She maintains her angles beautifully as she turns to the top [of her swing], building a tremendous amount of torque."[16]

Wie's swing has been admired by professional golfers and fans alike for its power and mechanics. She credits the development of her swing to her focus and extensive practice.

In fact, it was Michelle's powerful swing that earned her the nickname "The Big Wiesy," given to her by legendary professional golfer Tom Lehman. The nickname is a play on that of golfer Ernie Els, who has long been known as "The Big Easy" because of his smooth and powerful swing—a skill Lehman saw in Michelle as well. "She's got star power," Lehman said of the Big Wiesy in 2004. "She holds her head high. She walks like, 'Watch this next shot. It's going to be the greatest you ever saw.'"[17]

Michelle credits her swing to focus and practice—a lot of practice. As a teenager she practiced every single weekday for four hours a day. On the weekend she expanded that to eight hours a day. Her practice routine consisted of leaving school at about 2:30 P.M. and going straight to the golf course, where she played nine holes and practiced putting for up to an hour. At about 6:30 P.M. she headed home, where she did strengthening and flexibility exercises for half an hour and rode an exercise bike for an hour. Then she ate dinner, finished her homework, and relaxed before going to bed.

Still Just a Kid

Between the competitions and the daily practices on the course, it was easy to forget that Michelle was still just a teenage high school student. Even as she devoted hours a day to golf, she attended the elite, college-preparatory Punahou School in Honolulu. This is the largest independent school in the United States and boasts many famous alumni, including President Barack Obama. Michelle did well in school and maintained a 3.8 grade point average.

As Michelle moved further into her teenage years, she developed interests outside of golf. She developed crushes on actors Ashton Kutcher, Brad Pitt, and Johnny Depp, and she also loved Angelina Jolie movies. She also liked the television shows *Smallville* and *SpongeBob SquarePants*, as well as most of the programming on

Although she devoted hours a day to golf, Wie enjoyed other interests typical of teenage girls, including listening to music, reading books, and spending time with friends.

MTV and VH1. She escaped by reading, and her favorite books included *Seabiscuit: An American Legend* by Laura Hillenbrand and *Tales of the Unexpected* by Roald Dahl. Like most teenage girls, she loved music, and she counted Third Eye Blind, Coldplay, Bowling for Soup, and the Red Hot Chili Peppers among her favorite bands.

Bo and B.J. tried hard to make sure that Michelle had access to all the things a regular teenager might be interested in, like movies and birthday parties. She frequently enjoyed killing time by going to the mall and playing video games with friends. Although Michelle had some friends, she spent most of her time with her parents. Her parents' heavy involvement with her golf career, and the fact that she was their only child, enhanced her relationship with them. As a result, Michelle sometimes had trouble bonding with other girls her age. She knew she was more talented and more mature than other teenage girls. She also had little in common with other girls' day-to-day realities. As other girls navigated the challenges and dramas of high school life, Michelle navigated the successes and failures of a strong amateur golf career. She talked about tournament wins the same way her peers chatted about a hit song or a trip to the mall. When speaking about finishing ninth at the Kraft Nabisco Championship, for example, the young Michelle, who still wore braces on her teeth, declared, "It was pretty cool."[18]

Chapter 3

From Amateur to Pro

A s Michelle worked to balance a normal teenage life with that of a budding golf superstar, she wrestled with an important decision: whether or not to turn professional. The main difference between amateur and professional players is that professionals earn money from their games. Interestingly, not all professional golfers are exceptional ones—in fact, most professional golfers are golf teachers, golf course managers or owners, or experts who provide commentary. Only a small percentage of professional golfers actually compete for prize money.

Michelle figured a few more wins or losses might help her make a decision about whether or not to turn pro. So at fifteen years old, she started her 2005 season by accepting a sponsor's invitation to play on the PGA Tour at the Sony Open in Hawaii. She missed the cut, but played in five more LPGA Tour events that year. She also played in the John Deere Classic, a PGA event. The John Deere Classic was her third PGA Tour event. Although she missed the cut (by only two strokes), she generated impressive—and lucrative—interest and excitement in the event. *Fortune* magazine reported that ten thousand fans followed her around the course, and the tournament brought in 40 percent more in profits than the year before and vastly increased its television audience, too.

Michelle went on to qualify for the U.S. Amateur Public Links. In doing so, she became the first female golfer to qualify for a USGA national men's tournament. She impressed onlookers

Wie watches her tee shot at the 2005 John Deere Classic, her third PGA Tour event. The idea of an amateur teenage girl competing against professional men captured the attention of both fans and sponsors.

when she tied for first place in the thirty-six-hole qualifier and when she made the top sixty-four, which qualified her to play in the match. Although she eventually lost in the quarterfinals, being the first female golfer to qualify for the USGA national men's tournament boosted her confidence. The victory helped Michelle make the ultimate decision: on October 5, 2005, a week before her sixteenth birthday, she announced that she was turning professional.

"Bigger than Sports"

Michelle announced the news at a press conference at the Kahala Mandarin Oriental Hotel in Honolulu. The soft-spoken, fidgety teen thanked supporters for being part of her special day and declared her intentions. "The first time I grabbed a golf club

Wie announces her decision to turn professional at a press conference in October 2005. Her endorsement deals with Nike and Sony were estimated to be worth $10 million a year.

I knew that I would do it for the rest of my life and I loved it. Now, some 12 years later, I'm finally turning pro and I'm so excited," she said. "More than ever before I'm just going to practice harder than ever to try to become the best golfer in the world."[19]

Upon turning pro, Michelle signed with the William Morris Agency, a highly respected talent agency that deals with big names in the entertainment industry. William Morris does not typically work with pro golfers, but Michelle chose the agency because, with connections to the television, movie, music, and book industries, it had the power to make her a star beyond the golf world. "She is going to be bigger than sports," predicted David Wirtschafter, president of William Morris. "She will become a face and a figure in the world."[20]

Michelle also signed endorsement deals with Nike and Sony worth an estimated $10 million a year. These and other sponsors were highly interested in making the tall, dark beauty the face of their products. "From a marketer's perspective, Michelle Wie is a dream," wrote reporter Katrina Brooker. "Not just an incredible athlete, she's also young, beautiful, and perhaps best of all, approachable."[21] Others, however, thought these high-paying endorsements were a gamble, given that Michelle was not even officially part of the LPGA or the PGA yet (she either had to be eighteen years old to qualify for the tournaments or apply for an exemption, which she had not done). Some were even offended by the high level of interest in Michelle. "She's going to make something like $10 million?" said seventeen-year-old Morgan Pressel, junior golf champion. "For what? For winning one tournament?"[22] referring to Wie's June 2003 win at the Women's Amateur Public Links (WAPL) tournament.

Michelle was undaunted by critics and felt confident in her decision to turn pro. Even though she was not yet sixteen—she did not even have her driver's license yet—she had been competing in tournaments for over five years. She was ready now to see what the next level had in store for her. She made her professional debut on the LPGA Tour at the Samsung World Championship held at the Bighorn Golf Club in Palm Desert, California.

A Rocky Start

Unfortunately for Michelle, her first year as a professional golfer was less than glowing. In fact, some would even say it was disastrous. Michelle's debut as a professional was unexpectedly marred by injury, controversy, and poor performance. Critics began to speculate that Michelle was not yet ready for the challenge of professional play.

In October 2005, one week after announcing her new pro status, Wie was abruptly disqualified from the Samsung World Championship. The disqualification stemmed from a ball she hit into a bush. When Michelle could not find the ball, she dropped a new one near the bush, which is legal. She then hit the ball and made par on the hole. At the end of the round, she signed her third-round scorecard, which players do at the end of every round to certify that their score is correct. Even professional golfers sign scorecards, because it is nearly impossible to verify the number of strokes a golfer has taken unless the golfer officially records it. A penalty is given to any golfer who signs an incorrect scorecard, either accidentally or intentionally.

Wie speaks to reporters after being disqualified from the 2005 Samsung World Championship, her first tournament as a professional, for signing an incorrect scorecard.

Sports Illustrated reporter Michael Bamberger was watching Wie's ball drop closely from the sidelines, however. He reported to tour officials that from his viewpoint, Michelle dropped the ball closer to the hole than she should have, which is illegal.

Dropping the Ball

Michelle Wie's disqualification from the October 2005 Samsung World Championship for an improper ball drop marked the first of several mistakes that upset her career in her first few years as a professional. Immediately after her disqualification, Michelle sat down with interviewer Paul Rovnak to discuss her feelings about the incident:

Wie takes a drop after retrieving her ball from the bushes during the 2005 Samsung World Championship.

I'm pretty sad but, you know, I think I'm going to get over it. I learned a lot from it. It's obviously not the way I wanted to begin [my professional career] but, you know, it's all right. ... I don't feel like I cheated or anything. I felt like, you know, I was honest out there. And, you know, it's what I felt like I did right. I was pretty happy out there with what I did. If I did it again I would still do that because it [the ball drop] looked right to me. But I learned my lesson, I'm going to call a rule official every single time.

Quoted in LPGA Tour Media, "Wie's Post-Round Transcript with Officials," Golf Channel, October 17, 2005. www.thegolfchannel.com/tour-insider/wies-post-round-transcript-officials-17858.

Officials agreed it was not a good drop and gave her a two-stroke penalty. However, Bamberger did not report what he had seen immediately—he waited a full day. Thus, the two-stroke penalty was assessed after the round was over, and after Wie had already signed her scorecard. Since she technically signed an incorrect scorecard, Michelle was disqualified from her first event as a pro and lost what would have been a fourth-place prize win of $53,126.

The incident was controversial because to date, Wie is the only professional golfer ever to be disqualified from an event due to an error that was spotted by a spectator. Although Bamberger is a reporter and was probably paying closer attention than other spectators, he was not a tournament official. In fact, no tournament officials noticed anything wrong with Michelle's ball drop, and it was just due to random timing that Bamberger saw it. However, the fact that Bamberger was the only one to see the illegal drop, and the fact that he waited a day to tell anyone about it, did not sit well with many of Wie's supporters.

Bamberger was accused of deliberately waiting to tell officials so that Michelle would be disqualified. Bamberger denied this charge, stating that he waited a day so he could try to talk to Michelle about it first, not so she would be disqualified. "I learned a great lesson," Wie said of the incident. "From now on, I'll call a rules official no matter where it is, whether its 3 inches or 100 yards."[23] She tried to put a positive spin on the experience, saying that at least she learned the lesson when she was at the beginning, rather than at the end, of her career.

Unfortunately for Michelle, her debut disqualification was followed up by another disappointment when she shot four over par to miss the cut at the 2005 Casio World Open on the Japan Golf Tour. This was her sixth time competing against men, and it ended in failure.

Disqualifications and Disappointment

This series of mistakes and letdowns set the tone for Michelle's 2006 season, which began on equally unsure footing when she missed the cut for the Sony Open on the PGA Tour. Despite this disappointment, in February 2006 Michelle was ranked the third-best female golfer in the world by the Rolex Women's World Golf

Rankings. These were the first-ever world rankings for women's golf. What seemed like good news quickly turned sour, however: Michelle learned that she had not actually played the minimum number of required worldwide professional women's tournaments over a two-year period, and thus was being excluded from the rankings. In August 2006, after much discussion amongst the rankings representatives, the calculation of the rankings was revised and Michelle was ranked seventh.

As 2006 rolled on, Michelle experienced some brighter spots. She finished third in the Fields Open in Hawaii and finished in a tie for third in the Kraft Nabisco Championship, a popular tournament that is well covered by the media. In May she competed in the SK Telecom Open in South Korea and became the second woman

Wie poses for photographers after arriving in South Korea in 2006 to compete in the SK Telecom Open. She is extremely popular in South Korea, where her parents were born.

to make the cut at a men's tournament in that country. Michelle is very popular in South Korea and reportedly earned millions in prize money and appearance fees during the trip. That same month she also became the first female medalist in a local qualifier for the U.S. Open. However, she only placed fifty-ninth and also did not do well at the following LPGA Championship, where she tied for fifth. She also tied for third at the U.S. Women's Open.

The next few months were spattered with a few positive, but mostly negative, events in Michelle's professional career. Overall the period was marked by several subpar performances and withdrawals from tournaments. She lost in quarterfinals to fellow long driver Brittany Lincicome at the LPGA Hongkong and Shanghai Banking Corporation Women's World Match Play Championship in July 2006. Next she withdrew from the PGA John Deere Classic, saying she was suffering from heat exhaustion. Two weeks later she tied for second at the Evian Masters and tied for twenty-sixth at the Women's British Open, where she suffered a penalty for hitting a piece of moss on her backswing. Following this event Michelle's team fired her caddie without warning. Greg Johnston, who had been with Michelle since she turned pro, was caught off guard by the news: "I was shocked and surprised, I thought we had a successful year," Johnston said. "And I was extremely disappointed that no one named Wie gave me the news."[24]

Michelle's downward spiral continued when she came in last in the Omega European Masters on the men's European Tour. This was embarrassing considering the fact that tournament organizers reported that many of the thousands of spectators were there to see her. In Michelle's last three events of 2006, she performed poorly, even getting last place at the Casio tournament, an event at which she had done considerably better the previous year.

A Bright Star Dims

The second and third years of Michelle's professional career continued to be marked by loss, injury, and controversy. Not yet a member of the LPGA—golfers have to qualify and despite turning pro, Michelle had yet to qualify—Michelle was starting to feel the pressure of being a professional athlete who was not delivering

Wie pauses to rub her sore wrist during the 2007 Ginn Tribute. The injury caused her to withdraw from the tournament amid criticism that her real problem was poor play.

on her potential. She began 2007 by missing the cut at the PGA Tour's Sony Open in Hawaii in January. Shortly afterward Michelle fell and hurt her wrist while running and had to be put in a cast. She did not play golf again for close to four months.

Her next appearance was the May 2007 Ginn Tribute, but Michelle played poorly and ultimately withdrew from the tournament, stating that her wrist was bothering her. This caused an uproar among other golfers, who suggested she withdrew to protect herself from getting a bad score (according to LPGA rules, if a player gets a bad enough score, they are disqualified for the rest of the season). Wie denied this was the reason for her withdrawal, but she had trouble convincing others.

Michelle next played at the Evian Masters in July, followed by the Women's British Open, where she missed the cut. This was her first missed cut in an LPGA Tour event since 2003. Next came the Canadian Women's Open, followed by the Safeway Classic. Both

Top-Earning Golfers

Professional athletes earn millions of dollars through salaries, endorsement deals, and prize money, and golfers are among the highest-paid athletes in the world. In 2009, for example, in addition to being the highest-paid golfer in the world, Tiger Woods was also the highest-paid athlete of any sport, bringing in nearly $100 million. Close to the top is fellow golf legend Phil Mickelson, who brought in more than $50 million.

Annika Sörenstam was the sixth-highest-paid female athlete in 2010, despite having retired from the LPGA in 2008. Another top-earning female golfer is Paula Creamer, who brought in more than $5 million in 2010, despite having missed half the year due to a thumb injury. In 2008 Michelle Wie was ranked by *Forbes* magazine as the second-highest-paid female in golf, tied with Lorena Ochoa.

performances were dismal and were noted as such by the press. After Michelle's performance at the Evian Masters, for example, *Telegraph* writer David Davies commented, "This year, [Wie] has played 151 holes in a total of 62-over par. That is a truly terrible record for one who, when she first burst on to the golfing scene, was immediately hailed as the next superstar."[25]

In her first two years as a professional, Michelle floundered. By the end of 2006 she had only made the cut in one out of twelve tournaments involving men. She had failed to win any of her first nine women's tournaments as a professional. Withdrawals and gaffes caused her trouble in the first part of 2007 as well. As Michelle graduated from Punahou School in June 2007, her once bright star seemed to have dimmed considerably.

Although Michelle's professional life was not going well, she was excited to embark on a new challenge: college. Like family members before her, as well as her idol Tiger Woods, her dream was to attend Stanford University in California. She was shocked when she found out she was accepted. Wie described the moment that she and two of her friends read her acceptance letter in the computer lab at school: "They screamed, I screamed, we were reading the letter out loud, and everyone gave us these weird looks." She added: "It was one of my dreams, and I want to go through with it. I definitely want to go there and really try to graduate."[26] Michelle Wie entered Stanford in the fall of 2007, her professional career beset by criticism and doubt.

Chapter 4

Public Scrutiny

Few celebrities are able to dodge controversy, criticism, and scrutiny, and Wie is no exception. The fact that Wie showed enormous promise as a child but faltered in her early years as a professional generated particular speculation about whether she truly had what it takes to be a professional golfer. Since turning pro in 2005, Wie has been harshly criticized by sports reporters, journalists, and fans, all of whom have seemingly delighted in pointing out the ways in which she failed to deliver on the promise of her early career. Indeed, it seemed the world was just as quick to become disenchanted with the golf superstar's mishaps as they had been to become intrigued by her initial successes. By the time Wie turned eighteen, she had been called a has-been, a failure, even a cheater—all of this while trying to get through her freshman year of college.

Failure to Deliver

At first 2008 seemed to be looking up for Wie, but her optimism was quickly squashed by several mistakes and missed opportunities. The year began with her not being granted one of four available sponsor exemptions to play the PGA Tour Sony Open (this was the first time since 2004 that Wie was not granted the exemption). So she instead accepted a sponsor's exemption for the LPGA Fields Open, where she tied for a disappointing seventy-second place. She explored new territory later in the year when she competed for the first time on the Ladies European Tour, but she did not win, finishing in sixth place.

Wie plays a bunker shot at the 2008 U.S. Women's Open.
She shot an 81 in the first round and failed to make the cut.

A brighter moment occurred in June 2008, when Wie played at a sectional qualifier for the 2008 U.S. Women's Open. Her second place finish garnered her one of the thirty-five qualifying spots available, which was encouraging. But encouragement quickly turned to disappointment when she missed the cut after shooting an 81 in the first round, which prevented her from advancing further in the competition. This cycle of one solid performance surrounded by multiple poor ones seemed to be defining Wie's career.

A Critical Mistake

The summer of 2008 brought yet another crucial mistake that ended up costing Wie money and causing her embarrassment. After the third round of the LPGA State Farm Classic, Wie was disqualified for failing to follow one of the most basic rules in golf: She forgot to sign her scorecard. "I don't know why or how it happened,"[27] said a tearful Wie, who violated tournament rules when she left a score tent before signing her card.

Wie's mistake baffled her fans, frustrated Team Wie, and ignited a storm of criticism. *San Francisco Chronicle* columnist Gwen Knapp was among those who were outraged. "It might seem like a small thing, but that tardy signature spelled sloppiness," wrote Knapp. "This isn't how Wie was supposed to revolutionize golf. She was going to rewrite record books, not rules."[28] To those who argued the mistake was a silly technicality, Knapp and others pointed out that Wie had chosen to play a sport with meticulous regulations—respecting and abiding by those rules is a large part of the competition. "As a professional golfer, it is Wie's responsibility to know the rules," wrote sports journalist Brent Kelley. "And signing your scorecard? *Duh!* That's one of the most basic rules of all."[29] Golf expert Randall Mell agreed, explaining, "Golf's all about detail, precision, fundamentals. You can't skip the steps it takes to be a champion."[30] Mell suggested that because Wie had been fast-tracked to success, she had passed over important steps that were critical to a golfer's development. To Mell and others, it seemed that Michelle Wie was in over her head.

Dress Codes in Women's Golf

What women wear while playing golf has been a hot topic for decades. The debate between respecting the traditional, conservative attire and acknowledging that the game and the times have changed by wearing more modern and skin-revealing clothing that gathers attention (and, sometimes, fans) is polarizing.

The LPGA allows players to wear sleeveless and collarless shirts. While there is no specific rule on how long shorts or skirts must be, standards of decency are followed. Denim, workout clothes, and other clothing that is deemed disorderly is not allowed. At times Wie has been criticized for wearing inappropriate clothing during tournaments, such as skirts that are too short.

Though the rest of 2008 was not as disastrous for Wie, it continued to be marked by a string of mediocre performances, questionable decisions, and further criticism. Wie took more flack in August 2008 when, instead of qualifying for the Women's British Open, she decided to play the Reno-Tahoe Open, a PGA event. To many it seemed like an overly confident move for Wie to choose a men's event instead of a women's, especially considering she had yet to win a women's event. Since she was a little girl, Wie had endeavored to play against men. Yet given the other challenges she had experienced upon turning pro, sports commentators, fellow female golfers, and fans questioned why Wie continued to push to play in men's events when she was doing so poorly in women's events.

Golfer Annika Sörenstam was among those who commented that Wie should concentrate on qualifying for women's major tournaments before she tackled the world of men's golf. "I really don't know why Michelle continues to do this," said Sörenstam. "I think, if she wants to be a golfer, she should really concentrate on being on the women's tour and dealing with them and learning to win. Winning is what we are out here for, but I just don't see the interest really on being on the men's tour."[31] Some female golfers even took Wie's decision to play against men as an insult, believing that it was arrogant for her to compete in the PGA before winning in the LPGA first. As if proving her critics correct, Wie put on a disappointing performance: She ended up missing the tournament cut after shooting rounds of 73 and 80. In the world of women's competition, she finished out the year with a disappointing twelfth-place finish at the Canadian Women's Open, her final LPGA appearance of 2008.

Insult to Injury

During this time Wie was also harshly criticized for getting injured at what some suggested were suspiciously convenient times, such as when she was facing a loss or otherwise playing badly. She withdrew from the 2007 U.S. Women's Open, for example, claiming her left wrist hurt from an injury she sustained while working out in California the previous winter. That Wie was not playing

Wie favors her sore left ankle after making a tee shot at the 2009 LPGA Tour Championship. The injury caused her to withdraw from the tournament.

well prior to her withdrawal did not escape the notice of her critics. Fans were unforgiving and mocked her as she nursed her wrist on the course. "Give us a break, play through it!"[32] shouted one onlooker during the tournament. Wie was only seventeen years old and took it very hard. She put an icepack around her wrist and left the event.

Instead of resting her injured wrist, however, she tried to play in two more events shortly after. Unsurprisingly, she played poorly,

Most Common Golf Injuries

While it is true that golf is a no-contact sport, injuries do occur. Most professional golfers' injuries are related to the repetitive motion of swinging a club. Back pain is the most common injury. The golf swing, in addition to the hunched-over putting stance, puts great stress on the golfer's back. Golfers also endure golfer's elbow, which is pain inside the elbow and upper arm. Shoulder pain might be caused by a variety of injuries, including rotator cuff tendinitis, arthritis, or joint problems. Wrist injuries, like the ones Wie has suffered from, are also common.

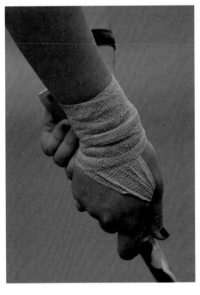

Wie wears a bandage on her sore right wrist in 2007. Golfers are susceptible to back, shoulder, elbow, and wrist injuries.

and she again claimed her wrist hurt. Sports journalists suggested she was using her wrist injury as an excuse for playing badly. "There has been a good reason for the waning credibility of Michelle Wie," wrote *Telegraph* sports reporter Oliver Brown, "and it has rested in the condition of her left wrist."[33] Wie's parents, coach, and agent all declined to talk about the injury publically, creating further speculation that Wie was making it up or overreacting. As *Golf Digest* writer Jaime Diaz put it, "The delay in supplying information and the lack of specificity added to the confusion and skepticism that often fuels reaction to events involving Wie."[34]

Wie claimed her injury was real and that she even had broken bones. She said these never healed correctly and affected her play in 2007 and 2008. "Everything hurt. I took a lot of Motrin. I was taking four or five pills a day, and then I had to take stomach pills because of all the painkillers. I even got food allergies, probably due to the stress. I got allergic to cherries, pineapple, dairy. I got sick all the time. I was not healthy."[35] Wie remembers being very upset during this period, both from the pain she was in and the lack of support she got from those in the golf world. "I would cry, then get frustrated at myself for crying, then cry some more," she said. "I didn't want to face reality. I was in a pretend world."[36]

In November 2009 Wie withdrew from the LPGA Tour Championship because of an ankle injury. Wie first hurt her left ankle stepping into a hole at the Solheim Cup in August, then hurt it worse stepping into a hole at the Navistar Classic in Alabama. Then she aggravated it again as she was signing autographs the day before the LPGA Tour Championship began. Yet test results later showed that there was no serious injury to Wie's ankle, feeding critics' speculations that she exaggerated her injuries.

Poor Golf Etiquette

In addition to suspiciously timed injuries, Wie's respect for the game was also questioned. Beginning in 2003 Wie had experienced run-ins with other golfers who felt her course manners needed improvement. At the 2003 U.S. Women's Open, for example, thirty-seven-year-old Danielle Ammaccapane, a veteran on the LPGA Tour, claimed Wie walked in her line as she prepared to putt and also moved around

A scoreboard at the 2007 Ginn Tribute indicates Wie's withdrawal from the tournament after the seventh hole because of an injury to her wrist. Many observers questioned the validity of Wie's injury and accused her of poor etiquette.

too much on the green, which is considered improper because it distracts other players. Angered, Ammaccapane reportedly pushed Wie on the green and yelled at her over the incident in the scorer's tent. Wie's father, who was caddying for her at the time, acknowledged that the Wies were inexperienced, but thought Ammaccapane overreacted. "Mentally both Michelle and I were affected by the incident. Her confidence was down,"[37] B.J. said.

Another time Wie was accused of poor etiquette was at the Sybase Classic in Clifton, New Jersey. It was raining, and many of the golfers, including Wie, were cold and uncomfortable. After completing her holes, Wie tended to rush on to the next tee box, leaving partners Paula Creamer and Hee Young Park behind. In golf, however, it is proper for players to stay on the green until everyone they are playing with finishes. While there was no official confrontation between the players, Wie's behavior did not go unnoticed. "That is Michelle's style,"[38] said Park wryly.

Perhaps the most famous breach of etiquette occurred at the May 2007 Ginn Tribute. Wie withdrew from the tournament just before the first round was finished, saying her wrist hurt too much to continue. The withdrawal was suspect because Wie was playing very poorly—she was 14 over par, and was nearing a total score of 88. The LPGA has a rule that players who are nonmembers (as was Wie at the time) and do not get below a score of 88 cannot play in any other LPGA event for the rest of the year.

Wie's score was putting her in danger of being disqualified for the rest of the year, and some speculated that the reason she actually withdrew was to protect her ability to play other events. Spectators noted she did not rub her wrist as if in pain, nor did she ask for any pain relief massage. "She wasn't holding her wrist," said fellow player Alena Sharp. "I think she just had a bad day. If it was her wrist, why wait until the last two holes [to withdraw]?"[39] If Wie did in fact exaggerate an injury to protect her game eligibility, it would be a show of poor sportsmanship—some would even consider it cheating.

Making matters worse, Wie showed up two days later at nearby Bulle Rock, where she practiced her swing—behavior inconsistent with pain supposedly bad enough to withdraw from a tournament just days earlier. Sörenstam was one of many who were suspicious of Wie's ability to play so soon after the withdrawal. "I just feel that there's a little bit of lack of respect and class just to leave a tournament like that and then come out and practice here," said Sörenstam. "It's a little funny that you pull out with an injury and then you start [practicing]."[40] Associated Press reporter Doug Ferguson agreed and compared Wie's behavior with that of other professionals who have withdrawn from tournaments because of injury. "[When golf legend] Phil Mickelson withdrew because of a wrist injury [he] flew home to San Diego for an MRI. He saw two doctors, had one cortisone shot and decided to withdraw from his next tournament," noted Ferguson. "Michelle Wie withdrew because of a wrist injury and went to the range to hit balls."[41] Wie said in her own defense, "I think it was very insulting because I tried my best. ... I think it's ridiculous to make any false accusations about me."[42]

What Happened to the Big Wiesy?

Most pro golfers have fallen victim to poor play, rules infractions, or questionable etiquette at one point in their careers, but few have experienced a rapid-fire downward spiral like Wie. The

B.J. and Bo Wie watch the action at the 2009 Solheim Cup. Some observers blamed the Wies for their daughter's struggles on the course.

string of bad play, silly mistakes, rumors, and scandals through 2008 left many wondering if Wie was washed up. Journalist Eric Adelson asked, "What had gone wrong? What happened to the 'Next Tiger Woods'?"[43]

While Wie's spiral drew strong anger from her critics, her fans wondered if her parents were to blame. Bo and B.J. have always been very involved and invested in Michelle's career, but perhaps, some suggested, they had become too involved. LPGA Tour veteran Dottie Pepper was one person who thought Wie's problems stemmed not from her demanding school schedule, her inexperience, or the rigorous LPGA Tour, but from "the greed and short-sightedness of the two people closest to Michelle, the people charged with molding her into a complete, independent and responsible person: B.J. and her mother, Bo." Pepper accused the Wies of "operat[ing] under a veil of secrecy and deception, even though they are surrounded by good people giving good advice, which they simply ignore."[44]

Tournament officials complained of the Wie's behavior as well. *Sport Illustrated* editor Jim Gorant noted that Bo and B.J. were told to back off of certain events, such as the 2009 Solheim Cup: "The ever-present B.J. and Bo Wie have been politely told that they will not be allowed in the locker room or team-lodging area, or at team meals. It'll be interesting to see how this affects Michelle."[45]

Still others speculated that perhaps it had all just become too much for her, that she had come to fame too soon, or that she was unable to blend her golf career with the demands of her class schedule at Stanford. Some, such as *San Francisco Chronicle* columnist Gwen Knapp, suggested that Wie had been overly coddled by the golf world. "Sponsors and LPGA officials have cooed over her like smitten grandparents. It has done her no good," wrote Knapp. "Wie remains a 13-year-old prodigy, stuck in an 18-year-old's body and an adult's endorsement deals."[46] Others, such as reporter Bucky Gleason, claimed Wie was the victim of media obsession and corporate greed. "Wie's childhood was stolen by sponsors and tournament directors who filled her pockets and lined their own under the guise of helping her development," wrote Gleason. "The public and media contributed to her fall, too, because we couldn't get enough. It makes you wonder: Is Wie to blame or are we?"[47]

Not everyone was so harsh, however. After all, she was still just a young girl who had been asked to cope with a level of pressure, stress, and expectation above and beyond the ability of most teenagers. PGA Tour golfer Joe Ogilvie was one person who thought Wie deserved more sensitivity. "Everybody is like, 'Win, win, win,'" said Ogilvie. "Chill out. Once she gets to winning, you'll get sick of her winning."[48] Rick Pledl, associate editor of *Wisconsin Golfer* magazine, agreed. "It's all rather absurd considering she's a 17-year-old high school student," wrote Pledl. "She may be a pro, but she's also still a junior golfer, and her future remains astonishingly bright."[49]

No one could deny that Wie's star had dimmed, even if temporarily so. "Her future once seemed limitless, her path to the pinnacle of women's golf inevitable," wrote *New York Times* correspondent Larry Dorman, who made a stark assessment with which both fans and critics would likely agree: "The reality now is that Wie is behind in her development as a world class golfer."[50]

Turning It Around

Everything Wie had worked for was on the line. When she stopped to think about the turn her game had taken—the injuries, the withdrawals, the criticisms, and most of all, the absence of a career win—she was faced with a stark portrait indeed. "I was fortunate early on in my career. I had it easy. It was a dreamland," she told one reporter about her career. "Then it all came crashing down."[51]

Wie knew she had to turn her game around for the 2009 season. To this end, she set her sights on playing on the LPGA Tour. Players who perform well in multiple tournaments throughout the year are granted automatic entry onto the LPGA Tour. Wie had not done well enough in 2008 to be granted automatic entry, however, so she entered a series of qualifying tournaments. She did very well, advancing all the way through to the LPGA Final Qualifying Tournament in December 2008. During this tournament Wie played well enough to become eligible for full-time play on the LPGA Tour in 2009. This was a career-defining moment

Wie celebrates making a birdie shot during the LPGA Final Qualifying Tournament in 2008. Her strong play made her eligible for the LPGA Tour the following year.

for Wie, and the start of a new chapter in her game. In addition to making the 2009 tour, Wie had completed over one full school year at Stanford, an accomplishment of which she was very proud. Things were looking up for her as 2009 rolled in.

Chapter 5

The Girl Behind the Golfer

At Stanford University Wie found a haven from the stress, pressure, and criticism of the golf world. She entered college in the fall of 2007 and attended school full-time in fall and winter sessions, taking springs off to play professionally. She has used her college years to explore interests and passions outside of golf, which have in turn made her a better and more relaxed golfer. As Wie has matured, she has also discovered she has an artistic and charitable side that helps keep her grounded when she is out on the course.

Just a Normal College Girl

Despite her fame and wealth, Wie's college experience has been fairly normal. During her freshman year she lived in the dorms, just like everyone else. "I just love the people in my dorm," said Wie in her freshman year. "Thankfully my roommate is pretty normal. I like her. ... So it works out."[52] One reason Wie chose to live in the dorms was for the company. "Being the only child in a house growing up, I never really had anyone to play with," she says. "And now it's like, on, I'm bored, entertain. You have 88 other people who are in the dorm. It's just great."[53]

At Stanford, she attends class, focuses on her work, takes careful notes, and asks questions in class when she needs to. She is a communications major but has taken a wide range of courses,

Wie relaxes in a dorm room at Stanford University, where she began her studies as a communications major in 2007.

including humanities, calculus, and Japanese. In February 2011 Wie had an article published in the *Peninsula Press*, a Stanford University newspaper. In the article, titled "Stanford Researchers Recommend Simple Steps for Curbing Childhood Obesity," Wie reported on a Stanford study about the link between childhood obesity and the home environment.

Wie is drawn to journalism and communications in part because of her unique, lifelong relationship with the media. She even credits classes at Stanford with helping her understand and cope with the media attention from which she has both suffered and benefited: "I have come to embrace it more through developing a greater understanding of the media," she said. "In particular, my communications classes have better educated me as to the process of journalism and how hard it can be sometimes!"[54]

Two Different Lives

While her friends at Stanford know she is a famous pro golfer, not many of the people she hangs out with understand much about golf. Most even forget she is famous. Said friend Casandra Espinoza, "To be honest, I completely forget she's a pro golfer. Then we'll be out to dinner in Palo Alto, and when people come up to ask for an autograph, it's always jarring. It's a reminder she

Wie chats with a fellow student on the Stanford University campus. She says that she rarely discusses her golf career with her school friends.

has this global following, even though she's just Michelle to us."[55] As Wie travels around campus, she stops to chat with friends and classmates, but rarely does the conversation ever settle on golf—and she likes it this way. "I kind of have two different lives," she says. "I love golf, but it's not the only thing in my life."[56]

Wie likes being able to forget about her professional career while at school. In fact, the main reason Wie wanted to go to college was to pursue a normal life. She wanted to have friends, parties, and boyfriends. She wanted to go to the mall, shop at thrift stores, and do all the things that she worried she would miss out on by not going to college. *Sports Illustrated* reporter Alex Shipnuck, who visited Wie's dorm room to interview her, noted how much Wie has downplayed golf in college. Her room resembled the living quarters of many college students—complete with tins of Spam canned meat, macaroni and cheese, and homemade artwork. "Conspicuously absent is any evidence that Wie, 20, is a well-compensated professional golfer," observed Shipnuck. "In every way possible she comes across as a normal college kid, from her wardrobe (short-shorts, sweet old school sneakers painted gold) to her nail polish (black) to her vocabulary."[57]

She tries to maintain a normal college social schedule and go out with friends as much as she can, though one major difference between her and most other college kids is that they are broke. "I don't even think about how much [money] I make," said Wie. "It's still an awkward concept for me." She says that when she goes out to eat with friends, "we still split the check, all the normal stuff."[58] Other normal stuff Wie does is date. She has had several boyfriends, including Stanford basketball star Robin Lopez, whom she dated in 2008.

Wie has successfully avoided many of the pitfalls that have tripped up other young athletes in the spotlight. She does not party a lot and is never photographed out at clubs or doing anything illegal (she says she did not even have a beer to celebrate her first career win in Guadalajara in 2009, despite the fact that she was over Mexico's legal drinking age). She enjoys adhering to the straight and narrow path of a young college student driven to succeed. College also affords Wie the chance to feel her young age. This is a welcome break from the maturity she has been

Stanford University

Located near Palo Alto, California, Stanford is considered one of the best private schools in the world. Founded over a century ago and formally called Leland Stanford Junior University, it is commonly referred to simply as Stanford. Students' primary emphasis of study is scientific, technological, and social science research.

More than fifty Stanford faculty, staff, and alumni have won the Nobel Prize. Admission to the school is highly competitive, and only 7 to 8 percent of applicants get in. Notable alumni include actors Jennifer Connelly and Ted Danson, broadcasters Ted Koppel and Rachel Maddow, and Google founders Sergey Brin and Larry Page. Golfers Tiger Woods and Tom Watson also attended the prestigious university. Because she takes a leave of absence each spring, Michelle Wie is on course to graduate in five or six years, instead of the traditional four years.

Hoover Tower is a campus landmark at Stanford University, where Wie is a student.

forced to display for reporters, interviewers, fans, tournament officials, her managers and agents, and everyone else who has had a hand in her golf career since she was a preteen. In short,

Wie loves school because it puts her right where she is supposed to be in life. As she explained it, "What I so love about college is that it allows me to be my age, to be 21."[59]

Wie is set to graduate from Stanford in March 2012. She is not sure what she wants to do when she graduates. Until that time, she will just continue to enjoy being one of hundreds of conscientious students who study hard, hole up in the library, pull all-nighters, and look forward to weekends. "It's hard work, but it's a lot of fun, too,"[60] Wie said of her college experience.

A Burgeoning Artist

When she is not studying, in class, or hanging out with her friends, Wie likes to experiment with art. She was first introduced to art by her best friend, Meg Akim, who thought drawing might help Wie relax. Wie was self-conscious at first, but eventually warmed up to it. She began sketching and drawing, using watercolors and even spray paint. Now she uses her artwork as a therapeutic form of relaxation and to express thoughtful, even sad, ideas.

Her drawings depict serious, sometimes disturbing images that have emotional and political significance. One drawing, for example, depicts a skull dressed in camouflage with snakes coming through its eye sockets. Wie was inspired to create this stark image after watching a report about the Iraq War. Other of her drawings typically feature robots: a robot attacking a teddy bear or a robot reaching for a butterfly, for example. "I think my life is so uniform, I make fun of it by drawing robots,"[61] she explained to *New York Times* reporter Karen Crouse.

Another of Wie's drawings depicts a sad-looking woman, with hair similar to the artist's, with a mouth boarded-up like a broken window. "She's crying silently, but she can't show it," explained Wie. "Sometimes when I just feel frustrated, when I'm not in the happiest mood, drawing is a way to express myself." Wie says that although some of her images are sad or disturbing, creating art makes her happy and helps her relax. "When I'm drawing, the rest of the world disappears. I think it just makes me really happy. It takes my mind off of things. When I'm stressed out, it's like a positive outlet I can go to to relieve stress. It puts me in a better mood."[62]

Wie sits at her desk in her dorm room, which is decorated with her own paintings and drawings. She uses art to relax and express herself.

On her blog, *Black Flamingo*, Wie not only posts pictures of her artwork, but thoughts about how the painting made her feel or what it is about. "Held up the brush again in my hand and it felt glorious," she posted on July 16, 2010, after she painted two canvases that feature a skull, a teddy bear, and the word *Perception* slashed in red paint across the bottom. "It was fun to take an afternoon listening to music while painting. took my mind off everything and i love how these kinds of activities just really reset my buttons."[63] For a person who has lived the majority of her life under the scrutiny of the media, it is understandable that Wie finds pleasure in escaping in an activity as personal and private as art.

In addition to drawing and painting, Wie likes to create her own jewelry and clothing. She owns a sewing machine and commonly experiments with creating designs for various fashions, such as T-shirts. She has also made her own leopard-print skirt, and even a leather dress. Designing her own clothes is not only fun for Wie, but therapeutic. Since her late teens, she has drawn attention for standing out among female golfers as young, pretty,

Wie's Personal Blog: *Black Flamingo*

Michelle Wie created her own personal blog in the summer of 2009. The blog is called *Black Flamingo* (www. ablackflamingo.blogspot.com) and Wie accurately describes it as "a mindless blog about life ... and the stuff that doesn't quite fit in." Wie uses the space to discuss and record her hobbies and experiences, such as her favorite songs, trips with friends, and outfits she creates. Other entries include pictures of her dog, Lola Taco, music videos and movie clips she likes, and general observations and musings.

Wie also uses her blog to document her love of cooking. She loves experimenting with vegan baking (cooking without using animal products such as eggs or milk) and posts recipes for vegan muffins, cookies, and other delicacies. Occasionally she makes a comment about a golf-related emotion or event, but mostly keeps her entries focused on the fun stuff.

and even sexy. She has been named to various "hottest women in athletics" lists and been photographed in bikinis and revealing dresses. Her physical appearance has been dissected, hailed, and criticized on various blogs, with some worshipping her as a beautiful athletic goddess and others criticizing her for being flashy and inappropriate. Wie views herself as a regular college girl who likes to dress in ways that reflect her mood on that particular day—whether it be via a skin-tight dress or a pair of beat-up sneakers.

Charitable at Heart

In addition to art projects, Wie devotes her spare time to giving back to the community. Charity has been a component of her life since 2005, when she donated five hundred thousand dollars to victims of the Hurricane Katrina disaster immediately upon

Wie hits a drive at the 2005 Sony Open. During that tournament, she participated in a fundraiser for the Kapi'olani Children's Miracle Network, one of several charitable organizations that she has supported.

going pro. Wie has also contributed to the Children's Hospital of Pittsburgh, the Hawaii State Junior Golf Association, and other organizations. She also created the Michelle Wie Foundation, which has given away $1.725 million to various charities since 2005. In one such venture Wie provided funding for a recreational room to be built at an elementary school in Hawaii that serves underprivileged and homeless children. Computers, video games, and air-conditioning units were among the items purchased with the money. "I think people don't realize there's a lot of poverty in Hawaii," said Wie of her home state. "When people think of Hawaii, they think of paradise."[64]

Wie's charity efforts are not limited to the United States—she has made numerous international donations, too. In 2006, for example, she donated three hundred thousand dollars to two Korean hospitals that provide medical care to poor children.

She made the donation a week before traveling to South Korea for the Asian Tour's SK Telecom Open, and she met with children at the recipient hospitals while on her trip. She has also donated to South Korean charities that are developing new technology for children with height disorders. "Wie sees her stature as a blessing and wants to help Korean children stand taller,"[65] explained *Golfweek* reporter Beth Ann Baldry.

In addition to giving money, Wie has played in numerous charity golf tournaments in which the prize money is donated to charity. When she was fifteen years old, Wie participated in the Miracle Birdie Club Fundraiser to Benefit Kapi'olani Children's Miracle Network during the Sony Open in Hawaii. Located in her home state, the Kapi'olani Children's Miracle Network supports the families of children who need medical care. It was the first major nonprofit organization that Wie attached herself to in her career.

Some might worry that going to college, making friends, having a boyfriend, creating art, keeping a blog, giving to charity, and having a life outside of golf might critically distract Wie from her professional career. Yet Wie claims her game has flourished from the balance the rest of her life provides. "I was so lost,"[66] she says, reflecting on the pre- and early Stanford years when her golf game suffered. Her activities at school and beyond have helped her find balance, self-confidence, and happiness.

National Collegiate Athletic Association regulations prevent her from playing golf on Stanford's team because she is a professional, but that is just fine with Wie. "Stanford is a chance to forget everything,"[67] her father says. Michelle agrees, saying her extracurricular and scholarly activity "puts me in a better place on the golf course. I finally realized why (amateurs) like to play golf," she says. "It's a great escape."[68]

Chapter 6

Going the Distance

Up until 2009 Michelle Wie's golf career was a roller-coaster ride marked by periods of impressive success but also dismal failure. In recent years, however, Wie has offered a more stable performance. Key achievements have cemented her as a golfing phenomenon, capable not only of hitting powerful drives but of controlling her game so she can win. She has also proved that she can bring a new energy to the sport of women's golf, energy that delivers a payday for Wie, tournament officials, sponsors, and everyone connected to the sport. On the personal level, she has demonstrated an impressive drive to push on through tough times, a respectable tenacity that is likely to help her enjoy long-term success in whatever project she chooses.

Beginning in 2009 Wie's golf game began to rise to a level that made both she and her fans happier. After finally qualifying to be a member on the 2009 LPGA Tour, she delivered several strong performances at a variety of tournaments. In August Wie was chosen by U.S. captain Beth Daniel to be on the American team in the Solheim Cup, a competition that occurs every other year between various American and European teams. Wie ended up leading Team USA in wins and points earned. Wie also received her first ever professional hole-in-one at the LPGA Championship in 2009, where she also tied for twenty-third, her best finish in a major tournament since 2006. Wie also tied for third at the Sybase Classic and tied for fifty-fourth at the State Farm Classic. But there was one event in 2009 that would prove most definitive for Wie: a tournament victory, at last.

Wie celebrates Team USA's victory in the 2009 Solheim Cup. In addition to serving as captain, she led her team in wins and points earned.

Finally, a Win

More than four years after turning pro, on the brink of being dubbed a fluke and a washed-up prodigy, Wie finally delivered her first LPGA tournament victory. In this significant win Wie overcame years of disappointments, setbacks, injuries, withdrawals, criticism, and negativity, proving both to fans and detractors that she was capable of a championship.

On November 15, 2009, at the Lorena Ochoa Invitational held in Guadalajara, Mexico, Wie beat Paula Creamer by just two strokes. As she realized her victory, Wie raised both arms in the air in a show of victory and celebration. She put her hand over her mouth, pulled her ball out of the hole, looked to the sky, and sighed in relief. Tears dribbled down her face. "I didn't think I would cry but I did," she said. "It was everything I expected and more."[69] Wie showed her joy a bit more ecstatically via messages on her Twitter page. "Wowwwww......never thought this would feel THIS great!!!!" she tweeted just hours after her victory. "I love life."[70] After sixty-five tries, Wie had finally won an LPGA event, which came with not only pride and glory but a winner's check for $220,000.

Sports journalists celebrated the victory along with Wie. Her win "fulfill[ed] the promise of a decade,"[71] wrote *Los Angeles Times* reporter Lance Pugmire; "What a Wie-lief,"[72] quipped the *Boston Herald*. Countless other reporters commended Wie for overcoming a six-year drought and starting a new chapter in her career. "The Michelle Wie era has, at long last, begun," proclaimed *Sports Illustrated* writer Alex Shipnuck. "Years of practice and preparation

Wie lifts the trophy for winning the 2009 Lorena Ochoa Invitational, her first LPGA tournament victory.

and want and desire were distilled into four nearly flawless rounds of golf."[73] Even Wie's opponents were happy for her: fellow golfers Paula Creamer (who came in second) and Morgan Pressel (who tied for third) congratulated Wie by spraying her in a shower of beer on the eighteenth hole.

Winning this event brought an immediate flood of happiness and also relief; Wie felt she had finally proved she could deliver on her much-discussed potential. "It's a huge monkey off my back. A huge gorilla, really," she said. "I'm really proud of myself for not giving up and pushing through. It has been so long overdue."[74]

Wie's play continued to improve, and she bagged a second career win on August 29, 2010, at the Canadian Women's Open in Manitoba. In addition to proving her 2009 win had not been a mere fluke (and earning her another winner's check, this time for $337,500), Wie demonstrated how much she had grown as a golfer. Wie's strength has always been long drives, but she won in Canada by making several key putts, showing off the strength of her short game. More importantly, the win cemented Wie's belief in herself. "I finally feel like I belong,"[75] she said. The comeback also bolstered public interest in and support for her. As ESPN reporter Johnette Howard put it, "There's no need to choose anymore between whether she's a champion or a survivor. Spread the news: Michelle Wie is both."[76]

Valuable Sponsorships

Wie's comeback has earned her not only big winner's checks, but sponsor's checks, too. Sponsorships are a way for professional athletes to earn income in addition to tournament prize money. Stars like Wie who are heavily watched can earn hefty amounts by endorsing products. Wie has slowly but surely turned herself into a brand that features a different kind of female golfing champ: one that is young, attractive, Korean American, and often outspoken.

Wie first attracted sponsorships when she signed with Nike and Sony upon turning pro. She also became a brand ambassador for the luxury Omega watches. Wie's LPGA wins have produced even more sponsorship opportunities. In 2010 Wie became the official golf ambassador and spokesperson for Kia Motors. Kia is a

Wie poses with a car manufactured by Kia Motors. She became a spokesperson for the Kia, which is based in South Korea, in 2010.

Korean-based automaker. Because Wie is Korean American, the automaker thought the partnership would be a good fit. Wie has appeared in several Kia commercials, one of which depicts her in a bright red Kia driving through a stuffy golf course. Wie turns heads as she cruises through the course, the music in the car blasting. The commercial gets at the essence of Wie: a young, untraditional golfer who has turned heads and challenged the norm both on and off the course. Wie is not only sponsored by Kia, but drives one of their models herself. Her 2011 Kia Soul is a White Tiger edition—tiger scratch decals run down the sides of the car. "I get a lot of second looks driving around the Stanford campus!"[77] she says.

Shortly after signing the endorsement contract with Kia, Wie won a two-year deal with fast food chain McDonald's. Wie agreed to participate in McDonald's-funded educational programs, as well as appear in commercials. Wie was attractive to McDonald's because of her multinational appeal—they saw her as a good person to help them break into the Asian market. "Michelle is relevant to an Asian consumer market that we're trying to penetrate and has broad appeal to young adults, women and the general audience,"[78] said John Lewicki, McDonald's director of alliance marketing. The first commercial featured Wie hanging out with friends in McDonald's. It was produced in five languages: Cantonese Chinese, Mandarin Chinese, Korean, English, and Taglish (a blend of English and the Philippine language Tagalog). It debuted in April 2010 in the United States, China, Korea, and the Philippines. Her commercial appears on a McDonald's-sponsored website called MyInspirasian. com. The site is intended to cater specifically to the Asian and Asian American communities. In addition to featuring Wie's commercial, the site hosts a page devoted to her story in which she discusses her admiration for McDonald's educational efforts around the world.

Sponsors like McDonald's and Kia love that Wie offers a fresh, multicultural face that appeals to consumers in overseas markets. Indeed, Wie is as popular, if not more popular, in Asia, and especially South Korea, as she is in the United States. Her South Korean heritage provides the foundation for a strong fan base there. Much of the country sees her as somewhat of a national hero who is putting South Korea on the international map. Bursting with pride for the Korean American, fans in Asia

Michelle Wie Is Lovin' It

Michelle Wie became the face of the McDonald's Corporation in 2010. Her first commercial for the company featured Wie hitting golf balls throughout her college campus. The balls are directed to her various friends, who are shown studying in the library, reading on the grass, or doing their laundry together. The balls bear the message "Meet @ our favorite place, MW." Wie and her friends are then shown catching up over french fries and burgers at a McDonald's restaurant. In real life, Wie says she and her friends from Stanford go to McDonald's about once a week to get food and hang out. Wie typically orders a Happy Meal or chicken nuggets.

cannot get enough of Wie. The fact that Wie speaks Korean also puts her in a good position to appear in—and profit from—countless foreign language advertisements.

New Talent Agent

This period brought other monumental changes for Wie. She and her team felt the new chapter in her life warranted a new public image. Shortly before winning the Lorena Ochoa Invitational,

Wie, posing with her dog, Lola, signed with talent agency IMG in 2009 in order to help rebuild her public image.

she dropped the William Morris Agency and signed with the International Management Group (IMG). The switch in agencies was rumored to be because IMG focuses on endorsement deals and other ventures specifically for professional athletes, whereas William Morris represents a broader range of clients. Plus, Wie just felt it was time for a fresh start, a big change.

With a client roster that includes other golfers like Tiger Woods, Sergio Garcia, Annika Sörenstam, and Paula Creamer, IMG is well positioned to resurrect the reputation of the child phenom who spent nearly three years immersed in chaos. "We have all watched the rise in popularity of women's golf, and Michelle Wie certainly is a prime example of the outstanding talent on the LPGA Tour and the bright future of the sport," said Clarke Jones, senior vice president and global director of golf clients for IMG, who was tasked with overseeing Wie. "Michelle is an amazing talent and IMG is delighted to be working with her and her family to provide the best management and marketing support in the world, allowing her to focus on her top priority—competing week in and week out on the golf course."[79]

Key Achievements

Now that she has bounced back and made millions from endorsements and corporate sponsorships, Wie is regarded as one of the most game-changing and influential people in sports history. Wie has long been a list maker: In 2005, while still a junior in high school, Wie made *Fortune* magazine's "Diversity List," which highlighted influential people of different races and nationalities. In 2006 she made *Time* magazine's list of the one hundred most influential people, an honor she shared with many world leaders and scholars.

Despite the challenges she endured in 2007, Wie ranked fourth on *Forbes* magazine's "20 Under 25: The Top-Earning Young Superstars" that year. Also in 2007, Wie made *Fortune's* "Top 10 Endorsement Superstars" list because, despite her dismal game, she still earned an estimated $19.5 million in endorsement income that year. In 2008 Wie ranked fifth on *Forbes* magazine's list of "Highest-Paid Female Athletes," with $12 million worth of agreements with Nike and Sony (the drop in earnings was

Wie crouches to line up a putt during the Honda LPGA Thailand in 2011. She finished the tournament in second place.

due to her wrist injuries and enrolling in college, which meant she played golf less often). She bounced back in 2010 when she made *Golf Digest's* 2010 list of top earners in the sport. Although Wie ranked fiftieth out of fifty, she was one of just three women to appear on the list. As of early 2011 Wie had earned more than $1.8 million in LPGA prize monies and millions more in sponsorships. Wie continued to earn prize money, bank endorsements, and improve her performance through 2011. She did well at the Dubai Ladies Masters in December 2010 and earned $140,000 in the Honda LPGA Thailand in February 2011 for finishing in second place.

More than her performance in any particular tournament, however, Wie has found a winning balance in her life. Passion for her sport and confidence in her talent has invigorated her, while school and life outside golf has grounded her. Each year she gains maturity and the experience that her older competitors have benefited from for decades. In 2011 she declared her intention to focus on playing women's competitions, which

Injuries and Penalties Continue

Although Wie's career was smoother in 2010 and 2011 compared with prior years, she continued to face injury and penalty. After experiencing some dramatic penalties and disqualifications over the course of her short career, Wie was again penalized in the final round of the March 2010 Kia Classic for grounding her club (letting her club touch the ground) after hitting out a ball of the water, which is against the rules. Although she heavily disputed the penalty, two strokes were ultimately added to her score. Had she not been penalized, she would have tied for second place and won $136,000. Instead, she finished in tenth place and only took home $34,897.

Wie reacts in frustration after missing a putt at the 2010 Kia Classic. She was later penalized two strokes for grounding her club, which moved her from second to tenth place.

Also in 2010, Wie suffered back pain from a disc bulge and two cysts near her spine. She had to withdraw from the 2010 Lorena Ochoa Invitational because of the injury, which was disappointing: This was the tournament in which she earned her first professional win in 2009, and so she missed her chance to defend her title.

garnered respect from those who viewed her desire to beat men as overly ambitious and arrogant. She has learned from the gaffes and etiquette breaches that marred some of her earlier performances, and she now gives a more even-keeled performance on the course.

The result is that Wie has come into her own as a golfer, respected not just for her remarkable potential but for her interest-generating talent. As sportswriter Eli Miller put it, "Sports superstars can be defined by how much they are capable of moving the proverbial needle, and right now, no female golfer shakes the ground in the United States as much as Michelle Wie."[80] Given her improving performance and confidence, Wie is likely to continue shaking the ground for a long time to come.

Introduction: "I Don't Want to Be Normal"

1. Quoted in Brian Murphy. "Girl with a Gift: 13-Year-Old Takes a Swing at Golf Stardom/Honolulu's Michelle Wie Has Lofty Ambitions," *San Francisco Chronicle*, July 2, 2003. http://articles.sfgate.com/2003-07-02/news/17498575_1_women-s-amateur-public-links-michelle-wie-lpga.

2. Doug Ferguson, Associated Press. "Wie Bit Off Mark," *BNET*, October 24, 2006. http://findarticles.com/p/news-articles/columbian-vancouver-wash/mi_8100/is_20061024/wie-bit-mark/ai_n51339956.

3. Tim Dahlberg. "Troubled Times for Wie at Open," *USA Today*, June 26, 2007. www.usatoday.com/sports/golf/2007-06-26-29130538_x.htm.

4. Quoted in Peter Yoon. "Golfer Michelle Wie Is Growing Up and Settling Down," *Los Angeles Times*, March 24, 2010. http://articles.latimes.com/2010/mar/24/sports/la-sp-michelle-wie-20100325.

Chapter 1: A Childhood Rooted in Success

5. Quoted in Guy Yocom. "My Shot: Michelle Wie," ESPN.com, July 27, 2004. http://sports.espn.go.com/golf/news/story?id=1847408.

6. Quoted in "The Golf Swing of Michelle Wie," Beau Productions, April 24, 2003. http://beauproductions.com/golfswingsws/michellewie/index1.html.

7. Quoted in Eric Adelson. *The Sure Thing: The Making and Unmaking of Golf Phenom Michelle Wie*. New York: ESPN, 2009, p. xii.

8. Quoted in Jennifer Mario. "Michelle Wie's First Coach: Twenty Minutes with Casey Nakama," TravelGolf.com, January 4, 2006. www.travelgolf.com/departments/clubhouse/michelle-wie-coach-casey-nakama-1521.htm.

9. Quoted in Mario, "Michelle Wie's First Coach."

Chapter 2: Little Girl, Big Wins

10. Quoted in Eric Adelson. "Behind the Story: Michelle Wie," ESPN.com, February 26, 2009. http://sports.espn.go.com/espnmag/story?id=3937168.

11. Quoted in James Corrigan. "The $10m Woman: Golf's Golden Girl Goes Professional," *Independent* (UK), October 5, 2005. www.independent.co.uk/sport/golf/the-10m-woman-golfs-golden-girl-goes-professional-509576.html.

12. Quoted in Murphy, "Girl with a Gift."

13. Quoted in Brent Kelley. "Q&A: Gary Gilchrist," About.com, July 21, 2004. http://golf.about.com/cs/michellewie/a/gilchristqanda.htm.

14. Quoted in Kelley, "Q&A."

15. David Lefort. "Els Up to Old Tricks at Sony," ESPN.com, January 18, 2004. http://sports.espn.go.com/golf/news/story?page=wrap040118.

16. David Leadbetter. "Swing Sequence: Michelle Wie," *Golf Digest*, November 2005. www.golfdigest.com/golf-instruction/swing-sequences/2008-07/photos_wie#slide=1.

17. Quoted in Doug Ferguson, Associated Press. "The Big Wiesy Makes It Look Easy," *Gainesville (FL) Sun*, February 2, 2004. www.gainesville.com/article/20040118/GATORS20/201180314.

18. Quoted in "The Club Kid," *People*, June 30, 2003, p. 132. www.people.com/people/archive/article/0,,20140447,00.html.

Chapter 3: From Amateur to Pro

19. Quoted in "Teenage Golfer Turns Pro," video clip of press conference, CBSnews.com, October 6, 2005. www.cbsnews.com/video/watch/?id=916789n&tag=related;photovideo.

20. Quoted in Katrina Brooker. "Michelle Wie Will Rock You," *Fortune*, October 17, 2005. http://money.cnn.com/magazines/fortune/fortune_archive/2005/10/17/8358083/index.htm.

21. Brooker, "Michelle Wie Will Rock You."

22. Quoted in Brooker, "Michelle Wie Will Rock You."

23. Quoted in Associated Press. "Wie's Disqualification Put in Motion by Reporter," ESPN.com, October 17, 2005. http://sports.espn.go.com/golf/news/story?id=2193534.

24. Quoted in Ron Sirak. "Wie Fires Caddie After T-26 Finish," ESPN.com, August 15, 2006. http://sports.espn.go.com/golf/columns/story?columnist=sirak_ron&id=2543475.

25. David Davies. "New Disaster for Michelle Wie at Evian Masters," *Telegraph* (UK), July 29, 2007. www.telegraph.co.uk/sport/golf/womensgolf/2317870/New-disaster-for-Michelle-Wie-at-Evian-Masters.html.

26. Quoted in Associated Press. "Wie Celebrates Acceptance to Stanford," ESPN.com, January 13, 2007. http://sports.espn.go.com/golf/news/story?id=2702418.

Chapter 4: Public Scrutiny

27. Quoted in Associated Press. "Scorecard Error Costly for Wie," *Los Angeles Times*, July 20, 2008. http://articles.latimes.com/2008/jul/20/sports/sp-golf20.

28. Gwen Knapp. "Wie's Sloppiness to Blame for Her Disqualification," *San Francisco Chronicle*, July 20, 2008. http://articles.sfgate.com/2008-07-20/sports/17174002_1_michelle-wie-lpga-officials-golf.

29. Brent Kelley. "Wie's DQ: Unfortunate, Harsh, Disappointing—and By the Book," About.com, July 19, 2008. http://golf.about.com/b/2008/07/19/wies-dq-unfortunate-harsh-disappointing-and-by-the-book.htm.

30. Randall Mell. "Michelle Wie Learns Another Hard Lesson," *Sun-Sentinal* (Florida), July 21, 2008. http://weblogs.sun-sentinel.com/sports/golf/bunker/blog/2008/07/michelle_wie_learns_another_ha_1.html.

31. Quoted in Associated Press. "LPGA Veterans Question Why Wie Is Skipping Major for PGA Tour Event," ESPN.com, July 30, 2008. http://sports.espn.go.com/golf/news/story?id=3510386.

32. Quoted in Eric Adelson. "On Path to Recovery, Wie Can Talk of Her Injury," *New York Times*, July 10, 2009. www.nytimes.com/2009/07/11/sports/golf/11wie.html?_r=1&ref=michellewie.

33. Oliver Brown. "Michelle Wie Aiming to Resurrect Her Golf Career After Long Injury Lay-Off," *Telegraph* (UK), July 23, 2009. www.telegraph.co.uk/sport/golf/womensgolf/5888699/

Michelle-Wie-aiming-to-resurrect-her-golf-career-after-long-injury-lay-off.html.

34. Jaime Diaz. "Wondering About Wie," *Golf Digest*, September 2007. www.golfdigest.com/magazine/2007-09/wie_0709.

35. Quoted in Adelson, "On Path to Recovery, Wie Can Talk of Her Injury."

36. Quoted in Adelson, "On Path to Recovery, Wie Can Talk of Her Injury."

37. Quoted in Eric Adelsen. "Potential for Controversy Follows Wie to Open," ESPN.com, July 1, 2004. http://sports.espn.go.com/golf/news/story?id=1832205.

38. Quoted in Ian O'Connor. "Wie a Ways from Playing the Boys," *Bergen County (NJ) Record*, May 18, 2009.

39. Quoted in Eric Adelson. "Wie's Comeback Doomed Right from the Start," ESPN.com, June 1, 2007. http://sports.espn.go.com/golf/news/story?id=2888679.

40. Quoted in Doug Ferguson, Associated Press. "Once Filled with Unlimited Potential, Wie Now Surrounded by Trouble," *Madera (CA) Tribune*, June 7, 2007. www.maderatribune.com/sports/sportsview.asp?c=216313.

41. Ferguson, "Once Filled with Unlimited Potential, Wie Now Surrounded by Trouble."

42. Quoted in Ferguson, "Once Filled with Unlimited Potential, Wie Now Surrounded by Trouble."

43. Adelson, *The Sure Thing*, p. 9.

44. Dottie Pepper. "Veteran: Wie Overexposed, Miserable," *Golf*, June 2007. www.golf.com/golf/tours_news/article/0,28136,1631997,00.html?cid=feed-tours_news-20070612-1631997.

45. Jim Gorant. "No 'We' in Wie: Parents Told to Back Off During Solheim Cup," *Golf*, August 18, 2009. http://blogs.golf.com/presstent/2009/08/no-we-in-wie-parents-told-to-back-off-during-solheim-cup.html.

46. Knapp, "Wie's Sloppiness to Blame for Her Disqualification."

47. Bucky Gleason. "Who Robbed Michelle Wie of Childhood?," *Buffalo (NY) News*, June 13, 2007.

48. Quoted in Erik J. Barzeski. "Sick of Wie Whiners," *Sand Trap.com*, July 17, 2006. http://thesandtrap.com/b/lpga/sick_of_wie_whiners.

49. Rick Pledl. "Let's Go Easy on Wie-sy," *Wisconsin Golfer*. www.wisgolfer.com/lets-go-easy-on-wie-sy.html.

50. Larry Dorman. "Wie Tries to Rebuild Her Game and Her Fame," *New York Times*, June 29, 2008. www.nytimes.com/2008/06/29/sports/golf/29wie.html?_r=1.

51. Quoted in Connell Barrett. "In Rare Interview, 20-Year-Old Michelle Wie Reveals How She Bounced Back in 2009 to Reclaim a Future That Looks Brighter than Ever," *Golf*, February 3, 2010. www.golf.com/golf/tours_news/article/0,28136,1957732,00.html.

Chapter 5: The Girl Behind the Golfer

52. Quoted in "Pre-tournament Interviews: Michelle Wie," LPGA.com, October 9–10, 2007. www.lpga.com/content_1.aspx?mid=2&pid=12948#michelle.

53. Quoted in "Pre-tournament Interviews."

54. Quoted in Eli Miller. "Michelle Wie," *Southland Golf*, March 2011. www.southlandgolfmagazine.com/t-People_Michelle_Wie_LPGA_Tour_Palm_Desert_Resident_Southern_California_Kia_Classic_Kraft_Nabisco0311.aspx.

55. Quoted in Alex Shipnuck. "Student of the Game," *Sports Illustrated*, December 7, 2009. http://sportsillustrated.cnn.com/vault/article/magazine/MAG1163428/index.htm.

56. Quoted in Shipnuck, "Student of the Game."

57. Shipnuck, "Student of the Game."

58. Quoted in Beth Ann Baldry. "Wie Delivering on Her Limitless Potential," *Golfweek*, January 1, 2010. www.golfweek.com/news/2010/feb/17/wie-delivering-her-limitless-potential.

59. Quoted in Lewine Mair. "Wie Revels in Double Life," *Global Golf Post*, February 28, 2011. www.globalgolfpost.com/opinion/wie-revels-in-double-life.

60. Quoted in "Should Michelle Wie Quit Golf (for College Life at Stanford)?," *Golf Blog.com*, October 10, 2007. www.thegolfblog.com/2007/10/should-michelle-wie-quit-golf-for.html

61. Quoted in Karen Crouse. "In Michelle Wie's Gallery, Artistry Off the Course," *New York Times*, March 20, 2010, p. B11. www.nytimes.com/2010/03/31/sports/golf/31wie.html.

62. Quoted in Crouse, "In Michelle Wie's Gallery, Artistry Off the Course."
63. Michelle Wie. "Perception Is Reality," Black Flamingo, July 16, 2010. http://ablackflamingo.blogspot.com/2010/07/new-thoughts.html.
64. Quoted in Baldry, "Wie Delivering on Her Limitless Potential."
65. Baldry, "Wie Delivering on Her Limitless Potential."
66. Quoted in Crouse, "In Michelle Wie's Gallery, Artistry Off the Course."
67. Quoted in Baldry, "Wie Delivering on Her Limitless Potential."
68. Quoted in Baldry, "Wie Delivering on Her Limitless Potential."

Chapter 6: Going the Distance

69. Quoted in Steve DiMeglio. "First LPGA Victory Gives Wie a Big Shot of Confidence," *USA Today*, November 16, 2009. www.usatoday.com/sports/golf/lpga/2009-11-16-michelle-wie-confidence_N.htm.
70. Michelle Wie on Twitter, November 15, 2009. http://twitter.com/themichellewie.
71. Lance Pugmire. "Wie Wins First LPGA Tournament," *Los Angeles Times*, November 16, 2009. http://articles.latimes.com/2009/nov/16/sports/sp-newswire16.
72. "What a Wie-lief: Michelle Wins at Last," *Boston Herald*, November 16, 2009. http://news.bostonherald.com/sports/golf/view/20091116what_a_wie-lief_michelle_wins_at_last.
73. Alex Shipnuck. "After Years in Spotlight, Michelle Wie Wins First Pro Tournament," *Golf*, November 18, 2009. www.golf.com/golf/tours_news/article/0,28136,1939582,00.html.
74. Quoted in DiMeglio, "First LPGA Victory Gives Wie a Big Shot of Confidence."
75. Quoted in Johnette Howard. "Just in Time, Michelle Wie Finally Arrives," ESPN.com, September 1, 2010. http://sports.espn.go.com/espn/commentary/news/story?page=howard/100901.

76. Quoted in Howard, "Just in Time, Michelle Wie Finally Arrives."

77. Quoted in Miller, "Michelle Wie."

78. Quoted in Adam Schupak. "McDonald's Signs Wie to Sponsorship Deal," *Golfweek*, March 22, 2010. www. golfweek.com/news/2010/mar/22/mcdonalds-signs-wie-sponsorship-deal.

79. Quoted in "LPGA Tour Professional Michelle Wie Signs with IMG," International Management Group March 18, 2009. www.imgworld.com/news/news/2009/mar/lpga-tour-professional-michelle-wie-signs-with-img.aspx?feed=news.

80. Miller, "Michelle Wie."

1989

Michelle Wie is born on October 11 to Byung-Wook (B.J.) and Hyun-Kyong (Bo) Wie in Honolulu, Hawaii.

1994

Michelle plays golf for the first time at four years old.

1996

At age seven, plays first eighteen-hole round and finishes 14 over par.

1999

Gets first professional coach, Casey Nakama; plays in first tournament, an Oahu Junior Golf Association event.

2000

Becomes the youngest player to qualify in a U.S. Golf Association amateur championship event at the U.S. Women's Amateur Public Links Championship; shoots a 64 for the first time.

2001

Wins the Hawaii State Women's Stroke Play Championship (youngest winner in history); wins the women's amateur tournament in Hawaii; wins the Jennie K. Wilson Women's Invitational (youngest winner in history); reaches the third round of match play in the U.S. Women's Amateur Public Links Championship.

2002

Becomes the youngest player ever to qualify for an LPGA tournament, the Takefuji Classic; wins the Women's Division of the Hawaii State Open; becomes the youngest semifinalist in the history of the U.S. Women's Amateur Public Links Championship; starts working with instructor Gary Gilchrist at the David Leadbetter Golf Academy in Bradenton, Florida; nicknamed "The Big Wiesy."

2003

Plays in the Kraft Nabisco Championship, her first LPGA major championship; becomes the youngest player to make an LPGA cut; becomes the youngest player (at age thirteen) to win any USGA title for adults by winning the U.S. Women's Amateur Public Links Championship.

2004

Becomes the youngest player to play in a PGA Tour event (the Sony Open); finishes in the top twenty-five in her first LPGA event of the year, the Safeway International; finishes fourth in the first LPGA major championship of the year, the Kraft Nabisco Championship; becomes the youngest golfer in the history of the Curtis Cup.

2005

Plays in the PGA Tour Sony Open but misses the cut; earns her highest finish to date in an LPGA event at the SBS Open at Turtle Bay, Hawaii; is first female to enter a U.S. Open qualifier; places second at the LPGA Championship; announces she is turning professional; disqualified from her first event as a pro, the Samsung World Championship.

2006

Honored on *Time* magazine's list of the one hundred most influential people; is ranked the No. 3 woman golfer in the world; becomes the first female medalist in a local qualifier for the U.S. Open; finishes second at the Kraft Nabisco Championship; makes the cut in the SK Telecom Open on the Asian Tour (traditionally men-only); becomes the first female medalist in a U.S. Open qualifying tournament.

2007

Announces she will not be playing in the LPGA Tour's two Hawaii tournaments due to a wrist injury; withdraws from the U.S. Women's Open; withdraws from the PGA Tour John Deere Classic; finishes second to last in the Samsung World Championship; ranked at number four in *Forbes* magazine's "20 Under 25: The Top-Earning Young Superstars"; starts her freshman year of college at Stanford University.

2008

Plays on the Ladies European Tour; finishes twenty-fourth at the Wegmans LPGA; misses the cut in the U.S. Women's Open; is disqualified from the State Farm Classic for failing to sign a scorecard; finishes twelfth at the Canadian Women's Open; earns membership on the LPGA Tour by finishing seventh at Qualifying School.

2009

Leaves the William Morris Agency and joins the International Management Group; wins her first professional individual tournament, the Lorena Ochoa Invitational in Guadalajara, Mexico; gets her first ever hole-in-one as a professional at the LPGA Championship.

2010

Wins the Canadian Women's Open on August 29, 2010; gets the second hole-in-one of her professional career; obtains sponsorships with Kia and McDonald's.

2011

Came in second at the Honda LPGA Thailand in February; had an article published in the *Peninsula Press*.

For More Information

Books

Eric Adelson. *The Sure Thing: The Making and Unmaking of Golf Phenom Michelle Wie*. New York: ESPN, 2009. Adelson, a sports journalist who has been interviewing Michelle Wie since she was ten years old, takes readers step-by-step through her career, recounting each critical match (both wins and losses) and analyzing her professional development.

John Andrisani. *The Michelle Wie Way: Inside Michelle Wie's Power-Swing Technique*. Nashville: Center Street, 2007. The author examines one of the most famous swings in golf today. Accompanied by detailed, step-by-step photographs from golf photographer Yasuhiro Tanabe, the book demonstrates Wie's swing.

Jennifer Mario. *Michelle Wie: The Making of a Champion*. New York: St. Martin's Griffin, 2006. Mario, a golf columnist, offers her perspective on Wie's life and tells Wie's complete story, from her million-dollar endorsement deals to her rise to success.

Periodicals

Beth Ann Baldry. "Wie Delivering on Her Limitless Potential," *Golfweek*, January 1, 2010. www.golfweek.com/news/2010/feb/17/wie-delivering-her-limitless-potential.

Connell Barrett. "In Rare Interview, 20-Year-Old Michelle Wie Reveals How She Bounced Back in 2009 to Reclaim a Future That Looks Brighter than Ever," *Golf*, February 3, 2010. www.golf.com/golf/tours_news/article/0,28136,1957732,00.html.

Jeff Chu. "Michelle Wie," *Time*, April 30, 2006.

Karen Crouse. "In Michelle Wie's Gallery, Artistry off the Course," *New York Times*, March 30, 2010. www.nytimes.com/2010/03/31/sports/golf/31wie.html.

Larry Dorman. "Wie Tries to Rebuild Her Game and Her Fame," *New York Times*, June 29, 2008. www.nytimes.com/2008/06/29/sports/golf/29wie.html?_r=1.

Larry Dorman. "One Victory Makes the Future Brighter for Wie and the L.P.G.A.," *New York Times*, November 16, 2009. www.nytimes.com/2009/11/17/sports/golf/17golf.html?ref=michellewie.

Bucky Gleason. "Who Robbed Michelle Wie of Childhood?," *Buffalo (NY) News*, June 13, 2007.

Gwen Knapp. "Wie's Sloppiness to Blame for Her Disqualification," *San Francisco Chronicle*, July 20, 2008. http://articles.sfgate.com/2008-07-20/sports/17174002_1_michelle-wie-lpga-officials-golf.

Lewine Mair. "Wie Revels in Double Life," *Global Golf Post*, February 28, 2011. www.globalgolfpost.com/opinion/wie-revels-in-double-life.

Dottie Pepper. "Veteran: Wie Overexposed, Miserable," *Golf*, June 2007. www.golf.com/golf/tours_news/article/0,28136,1631997,00.html?cid=feed-tours_news-20070612-1631997.

Rick Pledl. "Let's Go Easy on Wie-sy," *Wisconsin Golfer*. www.wisgolfer.com/lets-go-easy-on-wie-sy.html.

Alan Shipnuck. "After Years in Spotlight, Michelle Wie Wins First Pro Tournament," *Golf*, November 18, 2009. www.golf.com/golf/tours_news/article/0,28136,1939582,00.html.

Alex Shipnuck. "Student of the Game," *Sports Illustrated*, December 7, 2009. http://sportsillustrated.cnn.com/vault/article/magazine/MAG1163428/index.htm.

Sports Illustrated. "Q&A: Michael Bamberger," October 19, 2005. http://sportsillustrated.cnn.com/2005/golf/10/19/bamberger.qandq/index.html.

Michelle Wie. "Stanford Researchers Recommend Simple Steps for Curbing Childhood Obesity," *Peninsula Press*, February 14, 2011. www.penipress.com/2011/02/14/stanford-researchers-recommend-simple-steps-for-curbing-childhood-obesity.

Internet Sources

Johnette Howard. "Just in Time, Michelle Wie Finally Arrives," ESPN.com, September 1, 2010. http://sports.espn.go.com/espn/commentary/news/story?page=howard/100901.

Tim McDonald. "The Michelle Wie Phenomenon: Blame the Media—but Only Partially," TravelGolf.com, July 17, 2006. www.travelgolf.com/departments/clubhouse/michelle-wie-phenomenon-blame-2879.htm.

Randall Mell. "Wie Takes Her Hot Game Back to School," Golf Channel.com, September 16, 2010. www.thegolfchannel.com/tour-insider/wie-takes-hot-game-school-39522.

Darren Rovell. "Michelle Wie Wins, Now What?" CNBC.com, November 16, 2009. www.cnbc.com/id/33962852/Michelle_Wie_Wins_Now_What.

Stephen Wade. "Michelle Wie Wins First LPGA Tour Event at Lorena Ochoa Invitational," *Huffington Post*, November 15, 2009. www.huffingtonpost.com/2009/11/15/michelle-wie-wins-lpga-to_n_358510.html.

Guy Yocom. "My Shot: Michelle Wie," ESPN.com, August 2004. http://sports.espn.go.com/golf/news/story?id=1847408.

Websites

Black Flamingo (www.ablackflamingo.blogspot.com). Michelle Wie's personal, unedited blog about life as a college student, concertgoer, traveler, and regular young woman. Included are photos, recipes, art, and musings about life.

Michelle Wie Fan Website (www.michellewiefans.com). This site was created by fans and features updated information about Wie's wins and tournament statuses. Features a forum where fans can participate in discussions about tournaments, golf and non-golf-related topics, and more. The site also includes videos, highlights, and tournament schedules.

Michelle Wie Fans (www.michellewiefanclub.com). Another fan site that features forums, videos, highlights, and tournament schedules, and also a useful chronology of Wie's life. Links to other female golfers' fan pages are available.

Michelle Wie, LPGA.com (www.lpga.com/player_results.aspx?id=18563). This profile of Wie, offered through the official LPGA website, offers statistics, financial earnings, videos, news, an updated 2011 player performance record, and links to various other Wie-related sites.

Michelle Wie on Twitter (www.twitter.com/themichellewie). Tweets are provided several times a day by Wie herself, discussing how she is feeling, upcoming personal events and golf events she is preparing for, and other thoughts about world media events.

Miss Michelle Wie Website (www.missmichellewie.com). The frequently updated site contains all information relating to Wie. Includes a biography, photos, tournaments, news, and more.

Picture Credits

About the Author

Lauri Scherer has edited numerous titles in the People in the News series, including *Leonardo DiCaprio, Lady Gaga, Jennifer Hudson, Hamid Karzai, Katy Perry, Taylor Swift*, and many more. She lives in Ocean Beach, California, with her husband, Randy, and their son, Avett.